ENGLISH

KnowHow

Teacher's Handbook 2

Gill Adams

OXFORD
UNIVERSITY PRESS

Introduction

ENGLISH *KnowHow* Student Books

- progress over four levels from a beginning to a challenging intermediate level.

- provide balanced coverage of the four skills: listening, speaking, reading, and writing.

- are built around authentic topics related to people, places, and ideas from around the world.

- challenge learners to become aware of language in context.

- build confidence with clear, step-by-step language presentations and controlled practice leading to free and creative language use.

- offer frequent opportunities for students to express their own ideas in speaking and writing.

- involve students in the learning process by providing tips for more efficient learning and frequent opportunities for personalization.

- combine the best of the established and new in a coherent and logical approach to language teaching.

- address the practical needs of teachers and students in a variety of learning situations.

Know what is in this Teacher's Handbook

- General guidelines for using *ENGLISH KnowHow*

- *Unit overviews:* The contents of each core unit. Two aspects of a topic feature in each unit; ▶ indicates where the aspect changes.

- Detailed teaching notes for each unit

- *Optional Activities:* Suggestions for extra practice, as well as games and other activities that will provide a change of pace in the classroom

- *In the Know:* Notes with useful background and cultural information. These include, for example, additional information about some of the people and places mentioned in the text and about social customs, conventions, and language

- *Language Notes:* Additional information on the language of the unit and notes on common problems that students may encounter

- *Pronunciation*: Phonetic transcriptions for terms that students might find difficult such as names of people and places. Transcriptions for non-English words and names reflect typical pronunciation in American English.

- Answer keys (*AK*) for Student Book exercises

- Notes for carrying out the Keep on talking! activities in the back of the Student Book

- Workbook answer key

Know what else this series offers

- A Workbook with practice activities for each unit, Reading and Writing pages that build on material presented in the Student Book, and Check What You Know self-check tests to help students monitor their progress

- Audio CDs and Cassettes with all of the recorded material

- **ENGLISH** *KnowHow* web site: Go to www.oup.com/elt/teacher/ englishknowhow and sign up for the Oxford Teacher's Club. Here you will find the following downloadable items for each level of the series:

  -Classroom communication activities

  -Progress tests (one for each quarter of the Student Book material plus an end-of-course test)

  -A wordlist containing all new words presented in each Student Book and references to indicate where they appear

Know what is in the Student Book

The following unit sections are found throughout each level of **ENGLISH** *KnowHow*. Their order in the units varies, adding interest to the continuity within each unit and allowing for appropriate emphasis on different tasks as the units progress.

In Conversation

In Conversation sections introduce grammar points in realistic conversational settings. Students listen to the conversation with their books closed and answer a general comprehension question. They then read the conversation and check their answer. After completing the following grammar activities, students could use the In Conversation section as a model for further practice of the grammar in context.

In Conversation is just one medium used to introduce new language. Listening and Reading sections are also used as contexts for the presentation of new language.

v

Focus on Grammar

There are two Focus on Grammar sections in each unit. The questions that precede each chart highlight key points and encourage students to explore both meaning and form.

The exercises that follow move from more controlled to less controlled practice. The controlled exercises provide students with an opportunity to practice and allow teachers to check for understanding and accuracy. Freer practice exercises then give learners opportunities to experiment with the language creatively.

Language in Action

Language in Action sections present functional language to help students with everyday social interaction. Students encounter expressions in context and then use them in parallel situations.

These sections provide good opportunities for role-playing in a variety of social situations.

Vocabulary

Vocabulary sections introduce common words in lexical sets, as well as giving special attention to collocations, phrasal verbs, and words that may be easily confused. Activities clarify meaning, check understanding, and practice the vocabulary in a range of more controlled and less controlled tasks.

Once introduced, vocabulary is carefully recycled. Key vocabulary words from each unit are listed in the Vocabulary Reference section in the back of the book. (See notes on this section on page viii.)

Reading

Reading texts are chosen for their inherent interest and appropriateness for the unit content and level. Tasks provide both extensive and intensive reading practice. Students focus first on general comprehension. Then follow-up exercises check understanding of details.

Students are encouraged to deal with unfamiliar vocabulary as they would in "real-world" reading situations, by focusing first on key words, eliciting meaning from context, and using other strategies. Vocabulary is highlighted in activities before and after reading.

Questions at the end of a reading section provide further speaking practice, encouraging students to discuss the ideas in the text and express their own opinions.

Listening

Listening sections provide authentic-sounding recordings of a variety of text types that build students' confidence in their ability to listen to and understand English as spoken by a variety of voices.

The sections reflect real-life listening situations in that students are encouraged to bring their own knowledge and experience to the task and focus first on general comprehension of the main points. Successful completion of this task gives them confidence as they go on to listen for more detail.

Audioscripts are provided at the back of the Student Book for ease of reference. (See notes on page ix.)

Speaking

Speaking sections provide an opportunity for sustained speaking practice within the topic area. Students use the language presented in the unit and recycle previously acquired language. However, the emphasis in these sections is on task achievement and the development of fluency and confidence in speaking.

There are also many other opportunities for speaking throughout each unit. Focus on Grammar, Vocabulary, and Language in Action sections include oral practice, and Listening, Reading, and Writing sections encourage students to exchange ideas and opinions with a partner or in small groups. Many of these shorter tasks are also substantial enough to be expanded into full-scale speaking activities.

Writing

Writing sections help students develop writing skills and practice these with a variety of text types.

Most writing activities begin with a brainstorming or information gathering stage done in pairs or groups. This makes the writing process collaborative and communicative at the outset. Follow-up activities encourage students to read and comment on each others' writing, giving the task a sense of realistic outcome. Keeping the reader in mind also makes students more aware of the communicative nature of the writing process.

KnowHow

These sections are designed to encourage students to develop a better understanding of the learning process. Students acquire skills that will help them to reflect on the language and function more independently and confidently in English.

Among the aspects included in these sections are: tips on pronunciation, intonation, sentence stress and other aspects of spoken language; learning strategies, such as note-taking and vocabulary development; and speaking and conversation strategies.

In covering various language strategies and skills, these sections give students tools and tips to manage the spoken and written language efficiently and to become more self-reliant as learners.

Help Desk

The Help Desk feature serves to make students aware of aspects of language and usage and highlight areas of common confusion.

Review Units

There are four Review Units in each level. Each Review Unit contains additional exercise material to practice grammar and vocabulary from the units that immediately precede it. A special Recycling section within each one goes back to a grammar point presented even earlier in the Student Book or from an earlier book in the series. The Fun Spot contains a variety of puzzles and word games.

Know what is in the back of the Student Book

Keep on talking!

This section provides additional communication activities to accompany the units in the Student Book. These allow students to use the language of the unit in a variety of realistic and interactive speaking tasks.

Vocabulary Reference

This section contains lists of key words and expressions for each unit. These are listed alphabetically with the part of speech indicated after each entry. The "Word for Word" note sheets in the Vocabulary Reference section encourage students to write down other vocabulary items of importance to them that may come up during the course of a unit.

Grammar Reference

This section brings together information in the Focus on Grammar sections into easy-to-follow charts with key language highlighted in bold and additional language notes. There is also a chart of irregular verb forms for easy reference.

Audioscript

The Audioscript is provided in the Student Book for support and ease of reference. After completing tasks, students may wish to hear the recording again while following the audioscript, for example. Reading the Audioscript would also allow them to check answers independently.

A final word...

Enjoy using **ENGLISH *KnowHow*** and all it has to offer!

1 *All work and no play*

Main aims of this unit

Grammar: Review of auxiliary verbs; responding with *so* and *neither*; gerunds and infinitives

Vocabulary: Work and leisure; chores

Functions: Making conversation

Unit Overview	
Reading:	*How do you relax?*
Vocabulary:	Work and leisure
Focus on Grammar:	Review of auxiliary verbs; Responding with *so* and *neither*
Listening:	People meeting for the first time
Language in Action:	Making conversation
Speaking:	Making small talk
Reading:	*South Pole Journal: Frequently asked questions*
In Conversation:	"You really enjoy cooking, don't you?"
Vocabulary:	Chores
Focus on Grammar:	Gerunds and infinitives
Listening:	Being a child
Speaking:	Comparing the stages of life
Writing:	Describing a stage of life
KnowHow:	Learning tips

Before you start

If this is the first lesson of a new teaching period or with a new group, do the optional activity suggested below.

> **Optional Activity:** Write some words that are connected to your life (you can include names, dates, etc.) on the board. Tell students that these words are important in your life and ask them to try and discover what they are by asking you questions. For example, if you write the name *John*, students can ask *Is he your brother? Husband?* Keep it simple. This is not a grammar exercise. Then put students in small groups to continue the activity with their own information.

Warm-up

Ask students *Are you tired when you get home in the evening? What do you do when you feel tired or stressed out?* Help with vocabulary where necessary.

1 Reading

a • Work as a whole class. Ask students where they think the article is from: *A newspaper? A magazine? A book?* Have students describe the photographs and help with vocabulary where necessary. Ask if any students do any of the activities shown in the photographs.

b • Get students to read the article and say which answer is the most unusual. They will probably respond *Nathan*.

c • Have students read the article again and answer the questions.

> **AK** *Andrew and Charlotte relax alone.*
> *Charlotte and Nathan get together with other people.*

2 Vocabulary: Work and leisure

a • Put students in pairs to discuss the expressions and decide which relate more to work and which to leisure.

• Follow up by writing the headings on the board and have students dictate the answers to a student secretary.

AK   *Possible answers:*
Work: *have a long / hard day, do chores, work hard*
Leisure: *unwind, get together (with friends), be by yourself, take it easy, forget your worries, get away (for a while), socialize*

- If some students give different answers, ask them why.

b • Put students in small groups to answer the questions. Encourage them to use follow-up questions and comments.

- Circulate and listen, but don't interfere if students are communicating their ideas.

- Follow up by asking each group to report their ideas to the class.

3 Focus on Grammar

a • **AUDIO** Have students look at the chart as you play the recording. Pause at the end of each conversation to give students time to circle the final response they hear.

- **AUDIO** Play the recording straight through for students to check their answers.

AK   *I don't.*   *I did.*   *Neither have I.*

- Have students read questions 1 and 2. Ask volunteers for their responses.

AK   1 *Present continuous:* be
Simple present: do OR does
Simple past: did
Present perfect simple: have OR has
2 *The auxiliary verb comes before the subject.*

- Explain that these short responses with *so* and *neither* are used to agree with statements in the affirmative (*so*) and negative (*neither*).

b • This exercise could be done in pairs or individually and then checked with a partner.

- **AUDIO** When students have finished, play the recording for them to check their answers.

AK	1		*b)* *do*	*c)* *do*
	2 *a)* *are*	*b)* *am* OR *'m*	*c)* *did*
	3 *a)* *Did*	*b)* *didn't*	*c)* *did*
	4 *a)* *Have*	*b)* *haven't*	*c)* *have*

- Follow up by asking individual students for an answer or getting students to dictate the answers to a student secretary.

> **Optional Activity:** If your students are confident using *so / neither*, review the use of *too / either* here. Refer to the answer to exercise 3b item 1(c) and give the alternative: *I do too.* Then ask students if they can think of or remember alternatives for the other answers that use *so / neither*. 2(c) *I did too.* 4(c) *I haven't either.* Remind students that these alternatives (like *so / neither*) are only used when the speaker agrees.

> **Language Note:** *Me too* and *Me neither* are acceptable alternatives for informal situations.
> A: *I went for a walk.* B: *Me too.*
> B: *I've never been to Miami.* A: *Me neither.*

c • Put students in pairs to practice conversations 1–4. Make sure they change the information to make the conversations true for them. Tell students to exchange roles and repeat the activity.

   • Follow up by asking a few pairs to perform their conversations to the class.

4 Listening

a • Introduce the situation and brainstorm typical topics for informal conversation. Write all the students' suggestions on the board.

b • Look at the picture. Ask some questions, for example, *Where are these people? What are they doing?* Tell students they are going to listen to a conversation between Jessica and Adam, two people in a gym.

   • Look at the list of topics. Tell students to listen and number the topics that Jessica and Adam talk about in order. Tell them not to worry about understanding every word. They should just listen for the topics.

   • **AUDIO** Play the recording straight through. If necessary, repeat it for students to write their answers.

   • **AUDIO** Follow up by playing the recording again, stopping after each topic and asking *What are they talking about?* If there is disagreement among the students, play the section again. When the students have established the order of the topics, ask them what words or phrases helped them to do the task.

AK a *walking: 2*
b *where they live: 3*
c *jobs: 4*
d *the conference: 1*

c • Read through the chart with the students and check understanding. If any of them can answer before you play the recording again, don't accept or reject their answers. Just ask them to listen and check.

• **AUDIO** Play the recording again. Have students check the boxes. Ask students to compare their answers with a partner. If there is disagreement, play the recording again.

• Follow up by asking students for their answers. You could copy the chart onto the board and get students to complete it.

AK

	Jessica	Adam	Both
1 usually walk(s) outside			✓
2 live(s) in Canada		✓	
3 like(s) the outdoors			✓
4 live(s) near Phoenix	✓		
5 work(s) in sales			✓

In the Know: Vancouver is in southwest British Columbia. It is the third largest city in Canada. Tempe is a health resort near Phoenix, the state capital of Arizona, in the United States.

5 Language in Action: Making conversation

a • Look at the phrases in the chart. Have students try to remember the phrases used in 4b.

• **AUDIO** Play the recording and get students to check the phrases Jessica and Adam use. Follow up by asking *Did either of them say…?* and eliciting students' answers.

AK

Introducing a Topic	Asking Follow-Up Questions	Ending a Conversation
✓ Where do you live? ✓ Where are you from?	✓ What's (place name) like?	It was nice to meet you.
✓ What do you do?	✓ Where exactly is (place name)?	✓ It was nice talking to you.
What do you do in your free time?	Tell me about....	✓ I'll see you (tomorrow).
	✓ What about you?	

b • Tell students to fill in the blanks with expressions from the chart.

   • **AUDIO** Play the recording for them to check.

   AK 1 *What do you do?*
        2 *What do you do in your free time?*
        3 *Where do you live? / What's Mexico City like?*
        4 *It was nice to meet you.*

   • Follow up by acting out one of the conversations with one of the students, or getting two students to act one out.

   • Put students in pairs to practice the conversations, using their own information.

> **In the Know:** A graphic designer is a person who designs printed material, such as books and magazines.
>
> The word *scuba* actually stands for "self-contained underwater breathing apparatus." Scuba divers can dive deeper and stay underwater longer than people diving without this equipment.

6 ▸ Speaking

a • Individually or in pairs, have students brainstorm possible questions for each topic. Refer them to section 5 for ideas. If they are having difficulty, do item 1 with them. For example, *Where do you work? What exactly do you do? How long have you worked there? Do you like your job?*

b • Get students to move around the room. Ask them to try to talk to people they don't know well. Encourage them to find out specific information using the topics in 6a and the questions they prepared. Tell them that they should talk to the same person for at least 2 minutes. Make sure they begin and end the conversations, using the expressions in 5a.

• Follow up by asking random students to report the most interesting or surprising piece of information they learned about a classmate.

• **Option:** If the conference setting is not appropriate for your group, you could set up a different situation, for example, (a) Divide the class into two groups, the students at the school and the visitors to the school. You could prepare cards with information on them for the visitors to role-play. (b) You could create a party situation. They could be themselves or role-play popular celebrities. They could invent new personal information for themselves. To do this, they should be given time to think and maybe make notes before you start the activity.

7 Reading

a • Ask students to look at the picture. Have them describe what they see and what they think Nathan Tift is doing.

• Ask students to think of questions that they would like to ask Nathan. Write their questions on the board.

b • Tell students to look at the questions in exercise 7b. Read through the questions and check how many are the same as the students' questions in 7a. Make sure students understand the questions, especially *Do you mind the nonstop sunlight or darkness? What time zone are you in?*

• Have students read the text and fill in the blanks with questions from the list.

> **AK** 2 *What time zone are you in?*
> 3 *How many people live and work there?*
> 4 *What are your living conditions like?*
> 5 *Do you mind the nonstop sunlight or darkness?*
> 6 *What do you do for fun there?*
> 7 *How long are you going to be there?*

• Were all of the students' questions from 7a answered? If not, you could suggest that they do some research to find more information.

> **In the Know:** The time zone used in Antarctica is the same as that in New Zealand because most of the flights come from there.

> Because of the position of the South Pole, there is no night (darkness) in the summer and no day (light) in the winter.
>
> Volleybag is an adapted form of volleyball, invented at the South Pole because gyms are too small for the conventional game. It is played with a kind of cushion instead of a ball.
>
> There are several web sites about living and working at the South Pole. You may do some research if your students would like more information.

c • Read through the True / False statements with the students.

• Have students read the article again. The exercise could be done in pairs or individually and checked with a partner.

• Follow up by asking individual students (or pairs) for their answers. Ask *Why?* Do not confirm until they have given the reason for their answer.

> **AK** 1 T *(…to keep an eye on the weather.)*
> 2 F *(I honestly have no idea…)*
> 3 F *(…is fixed because there is no way in or out…)*
> 4 T *(I eat all my meals in the same building…)*
> 5 NI
> 6 F *(…all kinds of sports…indoor and outdoor…)*
> 7 NI

d • **Option:** You could review some of the expressions for discussion before this activity, for example: *What do you think? I agree / disagree with… because…. So / Neither do I….* Have students brainstorm expressions they might need and write them on the board.

• Have students compare ideas about living at the South Pole in small groups. Remind them to give reasons for their opinions. Also remind students about follow-up questions to keep the discussion going.

• Circulate and listen while the groups are doing this activity, but don't interfere unless asked for help. If there are any common mistakes, note them to deal with after the activity or in a later lesson.

• Follow up by asking groups to report the most common feelings to the class.

8 In Conversation

• Books closed. Remind students that a *chore* is something you have to do, often in the house, but that you may not enjoy. You could give some examples of activities you do. Use the expressions *I can't stand / I hate / I don't mind / I enjoy* to remind students of their meanings.

- Tell students that they are going to listen to a group of friends talking about chores and how they feel about them. Tell students to listen and answer the question *Do the friends agree on the chores they like and dislike?*

- **AUDIO** Play the recording. Let students say what they think, but don't confirm or reject answers.

- **AUDIO** Books open. Play the recording again while students read to check their answer. Check orally.

  AK *They don't agree.*

9 Vocabulary: Chores

a • Look at the vocabulary and the pictures. Have students match the pictures with the verbs on the list before they do the exercise: *take out, vacuum, iron, sweep, mop.*

  • Have students match the verbs to the activities.

  AK 2 *e*   3 *b*   4 *f*   5 *a*   6 *g*   7 *c*

b • Have students discuss the questions in small groups or as a class. Follow up by having a show of hands for the chores the students do regularly or that they never do.

10 Focus on Grammar

a • Read through the chart with the students. Point out the verbs that can be followed by either a gerund or an infinitive.

  > **Language Note:** A gerund is the *-ing* form of the verb used as a noun. When the *-ing* form is used as part of the verb in a continuous tense, it is not referred to as a gerund. For example, *I'm* ironing *a shirt.* (continuous form); *I don't like* ironing. (gerund)

  • Put students in pairs to refer to the conversation and find other examples.

  AK Verb + gerund: *I hate doing the dishes. I can't stand cooking. I don't mind ironing. No one likes taking out the garbage.*
  Verb + infinitive: *I never want to do the dishes. I usually plan to watch TV at the same time.*

- Follow up by asking some students for one example each. Then ask which two sentences could be expressed in a different way. (*I hate doing the dishes. / I hate to do the dishes.*; *No one likes taking out the garbage. / No one likes to take out the garbage.*)

- ***Help Desk:*** Read through the note and have students suggest more examples.

> **Language Note:** The verb *like* can be followed by either a gerund or an infinitive with little or no change in meaning. However, the expression *would like* is always followed by an infinitive. *I'd like to go out tonight.* Not ~~I'd like going out tonight.~~

b • This exercise could be done in pairs or individually and then checked with a partner. Make sure students give more than one answer where possible.

> *AK* 2 *doing*
>   3 *to finish*
>   4 *taking* OR *to take*
>   5 *to wash*
>   6 *to do*
>   7 *playing* OR *to play*
>   8 *to go*

c • Have students complete the sentences individually. Encourage them to write more than one thing. Ask them to use verbs, not proper names, after *love* (item 4) in order to practice.

- Have students compare their sentences with a partner or in small groups. Remind them about ways of showing interest and follow-up questions.

11 ▶ Listening

a • Look at the cartoon. Have students answer the question *What feelings about being a child does it express?*

> *AK* Possible answer:
>   A child's day only starts being good after school, when things are no longer so controlled by adults.

> **Language Note:** The expression *throw up* means "vomit." *Goof up* means "make a mistake." *Looking up* in this cartoon means "getting better."

b • Tell students they are going to listen to three children talking about some good and bad things about being a child.

• Look at the chart. Read the instructions. Point out that students don't need to write complete sentences. They should write just **one** positive and **one** negative thing for each child. (They will hear more, but at this time each person should note only one item for each category.)

Note: In this, and in all similar listening activities, students should not be required to write and listen at the same time. They should listen to a short portion of the listening text and then write notes or responses as needed. If students have difficulty understanding or remembering what they heard, play the recording again, possibly stopping after shorter segments.

• **AUDIO** Play the recording. Pause after each speaker to give students time to write notes.

• Follow up by asking random students for their answers. Make a list on the board.

AK *Some possible answers:*

Positive	*Negative*
1 play a lot, games (that mom and dad don't know how to play), play soccer	school, doing chores, cleaning my room
2 summer vacation, playing sports, getting lots of presents (on my birthday), playing with my friends every weekend, don't have to pay taxes	chores, doing dishes, can't watch TV (when my dad wants to watch a program that I can't watch), doing homework
3 don't have to work as a kid, my parents give me money (for allowance), see my friends at school, recess (so we can play)	having to go to bed so early, finishing all the food on my plate, older people telling me what to do

c • Look at the chart. Tell students to listen again and check the topics that each child mentions. Some topics are mentioned by more than one child.

• **AUDIO** Play the recording. If necessary, pause between speakers to give students time to check the topics.

AK

	1	2	3
sports and games	✓	✓	✓
friends		✓	✓
homework and school	✓	✓	
chores	✓	✓	
adults and work	✓	✓	✓
birthdays and presents		✓	
food			✓
paying for things		✓	✓

In the Know: Many children in the United States receive a regular amount of money from their parents called an *allowance*. Rules for using this money vary from one family to another. Some families ask children to earn their allowance by doing chores around the house. Others believe that doing chores should not be linked to the allowance.

12 Speaking

a • Look at the three stages of life. Ask students to think individually about the positive and negative points for each age.

  • Put students in small groups to share their ideas and complete one list for each group.

b • Work as a whole class to compare ideas.

  • **Option:** It would be useful to make a "master chart" on the board or on a poster. Each group could take turns writing one idea on the chart, being careful not to repeat any already there. This could then form the basis for the answers to the questions in 12b and help with the writing task in 13a.

13 Writing

a • Read the example text with the students. Tell students to choose one age and write a paragraph to summarize the positive and negative points. Ask students to write on a separate piece of paper, so that they can exchange paragraphs for other students to read.

  Optional Activity: Before doing part b of this activity, tell students to exchange paragraphs in pairs and help each other with language correction.

b • Put students in small groups to read each other's paragraphs and decide on the most popular stage in their group.

• **Option:** Have students post their completed paragraphs around the room. Get students to circulate and read as many of the other paragraphs as they can in four minutes. Bring the groups together to discuss the questions.

14 *KnowHow*: Learning tips

a • Put students in pairs to discuss the questions. Review their ideas with the whole class.

b • Read through the example suggestions in each category.

• Encourage students to think about how they can put the suggestions into practice. For example, *How can you practice speaking in your situation?*

• Put students in small groups to discuss and list their ideas for each category.

• Circulate and listen, but don't interfere unless you are asked for help. Encourage the use of English, but don't worry if the discussion moves into the students' language. This probably means the students are very involved. They should, however, produce their lists in English.

c • Follow up with the whole class to make a master list of the strategies discussed in 14b.

• Make a poster for each category and get the groups to write their suggestions on the posters. These could then be displayed around the room. More suggestions could be added as they come up.

• Have students reserve a page in their notebooks for each category and write the group's suggestions on it.

> **Optional Activity:** Suggest that students start a "Learning Diary." This could be a section of their notebooks where they record what they practice and when they do it. For example, after each class (or at the end of each week) they could note how much English they spoke, how many new words they learned, what they listened to or read, and how much they understood. This could be for both in class and out. They could also give themselves a grade for things like the amount of English spoken or the number of things they listened to or read outside class.

2 Making sense

Main aims of this unit

Grammar: More uses of the present continuous; stative (non-action) verbs

Vocabulary: Expressions with *get*; word building (noun suffixes)

Functions: Talking about language

Unit Overview

Reading:	Text messaging: New language or not?
Focus on Grammar:	More uses of the present continuous
Vocabulary:	Expressions with *get*
Listening:	What is your favorite word?
Vocabulary:	Word building (noun suffixes)
KnowHow:	Word stress
Language in Action:	Talking about language
Speaking:	Talking about your favorite words
Reading:	Synesthesia
Listening:	An experience of synesthesia
Focus on Grammar:	Stative (non-action) verbs
Speaking:	Talking about sensations
Writing:	Describing one of the senses

Warm-up

Ask students about their use of the Internet and cell phones. *Do you chat on the Internet? Do you use e-mail? Do you send messages on cell phones? Is your language different when you chat or write an e-mail? Do you use abbreviations?*

> **In the Know:** SMS (Short Message Service) is a service for sending messages of up to 160 characters to a wireless device, for example, a cell phone or pager. The recipient does not need to connect to the Internet to receive the message. People usually use an abbreviated form of language to send messages quickly and say as much as possible with only a few characters. This is known as "text messaging."

1 ▷ Reading

a • Have students read the messages and guess what the abbreviated expressions mean.

> **AK**   sup = *What's up?*
> h/o = *hold on*
> g2g = *got to go*
> ttyl = *talk to you later*
> c ya = *see you*

b • Look at the article and the picture. Ask students *What do you think this is about? Where is it from? A book? A magazine? A newspaper?*

• Set a short time limit, 2 or 3 minutes, for students to read the article and answer the question *What are the two different opinions on language change?* Tell them not to worry about new words.

> **AK**   *Dr. Ken Lodge thinks text messaging is fun, but he worries about the effect on children learning to read and write. Jean Aitchison believes these changes don't destroy existing language, but that they add to it.*

• Deal with any vocabulary problems here. Words you might point out are *evolve* (par. 2), *embellish* (par. 4), *clash*, and *embarrassing* (par. 5).

c • This exercise could be done in pairs. Check answers with the whole class.

> AK 1 ILB L8: *I'll be late.*
> FYI: *For your information.*
> IMO: *In my opinion.*
> 2 LOL: *Laughing out loud* OR *Lots of love.*

d • Put students in pairs or small groups to discuss the questions. Circulate and listen, but don't interfere unless you are asked for help. Feedback with the whole group.

• If students have given examples of English words that have entered their own language, it could be interesting to compare the original meaning in English with the meaning in their language.

2 ▶ Focus on Grammar

a • Have students read the sentences and choose those that refer to situations that are happening *right now* and *around now*.

> AK Right now: *1 and 4*
> Around now: *2 and 3*

b • Have students refer back to the article on page 9 to find at least two examples of the present continuous for changing or developing situations. This could be done in pairs or individually and then compared with a partner.

> AK *Text messaging is affecting language.* / *...the language is...evolving* / *We are composing a new aspect of vocabulary and (we are) opening up...* / *...what is happening to good old-fashioned English?*

Note: The expression "good old-fashioned" is idiomatic for "traditional" or "standard."

• Negative and question formation are shown in the Grammar Reference at the back of the book.

c • Read the example and get students to suggest other possible sentences for item 1.

• Have students write sentences for 1–4 individually. Then put students in pairs or small groups to compare their answers.

> AK *Answers will vary, but check that students have formed the present continuous verbs correctly and that the sentences are appropriate for the situations.*

• Follow up by asking students for the most interesting or surprising answer they heard.

3 Vocabulary: Expressions with *get*

a • Look at the diagrams. Read the examples with the students. Have students complete the diagrams with the phrases in bold.

> **AK** become: *get better, get angry*
> obtain or receive: *get a letter, get some new clothes*
> arrive: *get home, get there*

b • This exercise could be done in pairs or individually and then checked with a partner. Remind students to think about the correct form of the expressions.

• Feedback with the whole group.

> **AK** 2 *get new clothes*
> 3 *getting bigger*
> 4 *get here*
> 5 *get a taxi*
> 6 *gets a newspaper*

> **Optional Activity:** Have a group discussion about things that are changing in the world today. Brainstorm topics with the students, for example, climate, entertainment, or education. Get students to make groups according to the topic that interests them. Ask them to discuss what is changing and produce a diagram with the topic in the center and the changes around it. Tell them that each group will present their diagram to the rest of the class. Set a time limit of ten minutes. The diagrams could then be displayed and each group could give an oral presentation explaining them.

4 Listening

a • Look at the list of words and expressions and the illustrations. Ask students which ones they recognize. Tell students not to worry about those they don't recognize at this time. This will be the subject of the listening activity.

b • Tell students they are going to listen to six people talking about their favorite words and expressions.

• Look at the chart. Tell students to listen and write the words or expressions that each person mentions. They should not worry about the *Reason* column at this stage.

• **AUDIO** Play the recording, pausing after each speaker to give students time to write the words.

- **AUDIO** Play the recording again if necessary. You could get students to compare answers with a partner before the follow-up with the group.

c • Tell students to listen again and make notes in the *Reason* column. They don't need to write complete sentences, just words that will help them remember the reasons.

- **AUDIO** Play the recording, pausing after each speaker to give students time to write. Follow up as in b.

AK		
Silvia	*hectic, forward*	*the sound, the meaning*
Victor	*imagination*	*both meaning and sound*
Fabiana	*strength*	*only one vowel and seven consonants, likes to pronounce it, likes its meaning*
Takahiro	*flabbergasted*	*almost like you can see what it means*
Anna	*happiness, fabulous, "come easy"*	*meaning, thought it was just one word*
Alfredo	*curiosity, "Curiosity killed the cat"*	*both sound and meaning, funny expression (to say that too much curiosity can be a bad thing)*

- Ask students if there are still any words they don't understand. If there are, provide explanations.

- If necessary, practice the pronunciation of *flabbergasted* /ˈflæbərgæstəd/, *strength* /strɛŋkθ/, and *curiosity* /ˌkyʊriˈɑsəti/.

d • Ask students which of these words they like best. Have a show of hands for each word or expression. Ask random students for their reasons.

5 ▷ Vocabulary: Word building (noun suffixes)

a • Look at the examples. Ask students *What are the four suffixes?*

> *AK* -ness   -ity   -ment   -ation

- After checking the answers, you could point out that the suffixes -*ness* and -*ity* indicate the formation of nouns from adjectives and -*ment* and -*ation* of nouns from verbs. Make it clear, however, that there are no absolute rules for knowing when to use which suffix. Even native English speakers sometimes have to check the dictionary to know which form to use.

• Look at the spelling. Ask students to identify the spelling changes.

> **AK** *The letter* y *changes to* i *before the ending* -ness. *The letters* ous *change to* os *before the ending* -ity. *Words ending in* -ine *drop the* -e *before adding* -ation.

b • Have students form the nouns and put them into the correct columns. This could be done in pairs.

• Follow up by copying the chart onto the board and getting individual students to write the nouns into the columns.

AK

(1) -ness	*(2)* -ity	*(3)* -ment	*(4)* -ation
happiness	curiosity	excitement	imagination
kindness	creativity	achievement	education
darkness	stupidity	management	exploration
goodness	similarity	government	celebration
sleepiness	possibility		translation
sadness			

Pronunciation: similarity /ˌsɪməˈlærəti/   management /ˈmænɪdʒmənt/

Optional Activity: If appropriate, you could compare the suffixes in English with equivalent suffixes in the students' language. This could help students to make intelligent guesses at the formation of other nouns.

c • Look at the example (item 1). Check that students understand what they are to do. Have students complete sentences 2–6.

• Follow up by asking individual students for their answers. Ask *How do you spell that?* to check the spelling.

> **AK** 2 *curiosity*
> 3 *possibility*
> 4 *similarity*
> 5 *creativity*
> 6 *achievements*

6 ▸ *KnowHow* : Word stress

a • **AUDIO** Look at the words. Play the recording. Have students listen for the stress on the words as indicated by the dots.

> **AK** *The stress comes on the syllable before* -ity *and on the* a *of* -ation.

• **AUDIO** Play the recording again, pause after each pair and have students repeat the words. If necessary, tap out the rhythm of the word or clap your hands on the stressed syllable.

b • **AUDIO** Have students mark the stress on the words given and then try to say them, working either as a whole group or in pairs. Encourage them to find similar words in 6a and use them as models. If students are working in pairs, circulate and check.

Note: Keep this part of the activity short. If students are making mistakes, they shouldn't be allowed to "practice" the mistakes for long.

• **AUDIO** Play the recording so that students can check their pronunciation. They should then practice saying the words correctly with the recording.

> **AK** exploration   similarity   possibility
> translation   education   stupidity

c • Put students in pairs. Ask students if they can add three more words for each ending. Encourage them to experiment with building nouns from the verbs and adjectives they know. Have students compare answers with a partner.

> **AK** *Possible answers:*
> *generous-generosity, real-reality, communicate-communication, careful-carefulness, disappoint-disappointment*

7 ▸ Language in Action: Talking about language

a • Have students look at the picture and describe it. Ask students some questions, for example, *Who are these people?* (Victor and Silvia from the listening activity in 4.) *What are they doing? What do you think they're talking about?*

• **AUDIO** Tell students they are going to listen to the conversation. They should answer the question *What word are Victor and Silvia talking about?* Play the recording straight through.

> **AK** *They're talking about the word* flabbergasted.

b • [AUDIO] Have students look at the questions in the list and then listen again and check (✓) the questions Victor asks.

> [AK] ✓ What does this word mean?   ✓ Is it a noun?
> ✓ How do you pronounce it?   ✓ Is it a formal word?

c • Read through the example. Put students in pairs to make their own conversations. Tell them to take turns asking the questions from exercise 7b. Circulate and listen.

• Follow up by asking random pairs to repeat one of their conversations for the whole group.

• **Option:** Have students continue asking each other about other English words they may have seen or heard but don't know the meaning of.

8 Speaking

a • Have students work in small groups to exchange information and complete the chart. Tell students you are going to ask each group to report to the whole class.

• **Option:** Give each group a large piece of paper to write their results on. This can then be shown to the whole class during the follow up.

Note: It often works better if the group has only one chart to complete, as this prevents students from working individually instead of as a group.

b • Follow up by asking each group to report the favorite words and expressions they discovered. You could ask students to write these on the board. If they have made the charts on large pieces of paper, these could be posted around the room. The students could then circulate and read the other groups' words.

• Bring the groups together to report words that are repeated in different charts and to check the meaning of any new words. If there are any new words, students should ask the person whose favorite word it is to explain the meaning.

9 Reading

a • Look at the lists of words. Have students match the verbs to the parts of the body. If necessary, mime actions to help them.

> [AK] 2 c   3 e   4 a   5 b

> **Language Note:** The meaning of the word *orderly*, as used in this article, is "clearly defined or separated." For people with synesthesia, the senses are not clearly separated from one another. For example, music may be both heard and seen.

- **Help Desk:** Read through the Help Desk with the students. Ask students if there are similar pairs of verbs in their language.

> **Language Note:** *vs.* is an abbreviation for the word *versus* which means "as opposed to" or "in contrast to." It is also commonly abbreviated using the single letter *v.*
>
> *Watch* and *look at* are slightly different. *Watch* is often used to talk about something which has movement, for example, a football game or a movie.

> **Optional Activity:** Ask students what they can hear at the moment (*noises from outside the room?*), and then ask them what they are listening to (*your voice?*). Ask students to look at you and then ask them what else they can see (*the board? the table?*). Ask students if they can think of more examples. For example, *I like to listen to music. I can hear the noise of the traffic outside. I'm looking at my book. I can see the desk.*

b • Tell students they are going to read an article about *synesthesia* /ˌsɪnɪsˈθiʒə/. They should read the article quickly—set a time limit of about 2 minutes—and answer the two questions. Tell them not to worry about words they don't understand as they will be working on the vocabulary later.

> *AK* *Synesthesia is a phenomenon that occurs when two or more senses mix together. Not all people who experience synesthesia describe it the same way.*

> **In the Know:** Vladimir Nabokov /ˈnɑbəˌkɔf/ (1899–1977) was the author of *Lolita* (1958).
>
> A neuroscientist /ˌnʊroʊˈsaɪəntɪst/ studies how the brain works.

> **Pronunciation:** phenomenon /fəˈnɑmənɑn/
>   Grossenbacher /ˌgroʊsənˈbɑkər/

c • Tell students to read the article in detail to complete the exercise. They could compare their answers with a partner before following up with the whole class.

• Ask random students for their answers.

> **AK** 1 *a musical note that tastes like pickles; the sound of a guitar that*
>   *feels like a soft touch...*
>   2 *the color of the letter L*
>   3 *an illness, artistically gifted, not believed*
>   4 *synesthesia seems to run in families; it is more common in women*
>   *than men; it is an international phenomenon*

d • Tell students to find each word in the text and re-read the sentence that
it occurs in before choosing the definition. They could work in pairs.

• Follow up by asking random students (or pairs) for their answers and
their reasons.

> **AK** 2 *d*   3 *g*   4 *f*   5 *c*   6 *e*   7 *a*

e • Ask the whole group the question. If anyone has known or heard of a
person with synesthesia, ask them if they can, to give some examples of
the experience.

10 Listening

a • Tell students they are going to listen to a person talking about her
experience of synesthesia.

• Have students describe the picture and ask the question *What do you*
think this person's experience is related to? (Days of the week and colors.)

b • **AUDIO** Read the questions with the students. Tell them to listen to find
the answers. Remind them not to worry about details at this stage. Play
the recording straight through.

• Ask students for any information or ideas they heard that might help
answer the questions. Write their contributions on the board. If students
can't put together enough information to answer the questions, play the
recording again and pause at key points.

> **AK** 1 *She experienced it as a child.*
>   2 *It's nice. / It would be great fun to experience more of it now.*

c • Look at the chart. Read through the words and phrases, check
understanding and pronunciation, especially *lilac* /ˈlaɪ.lɑk/ and *ballet*
/bæˈleɪ/.

• **AUDIO** Tell students to listen again and put the words with the correct
days of the week. If any of them can do some from memory, tell students
to write them in and then listen to check their answers.

	Monday	Tuesday	Wednesday	Thursday
AK	brown lilac clouds	blue	ballet teacher red velvet curtain a stage	orange

Friday	Saturday	Sunday
bright yellow	gray	red rectangle

> **In the Know:** Lilac is a pale, pinkish purple color. The word comes from the name of a tree that has this color flowers. Velvet is a soft, finely woven fabric with a furry surface on one side.

- **AUDIO** Follow up by asking random students for their answers. If there is disagreement or uncertainty, play the recording again, pausing after each day of the week for students to check.

d • Ask students to give their opinions in small groups or as a whole class.

11 ▶ Focus on Grammar

a • Read through the chart with the students. Have students circle the stative verbs on the list.

    AK *understand   need   love   sound*

Note: Read through the note with the students and have them make more examples. For example, *This soup tastes good. I'm tasting this soup to see if it needs more salt. I think this exercise is easy. I'm thinking of going to Spain next year.*

> **Language Note:** The verbs *like* and *love* can also be used in the present continuous when referring to a **temporary** state. For example: I *love* parties. (in general) vs. *I'm loving* this party. (at this moment) OR *I like* school. vs. *I'm liking* this school much better now.

b • Have students look back at the article on page 13 to find more examples of stative verbs.

> *AK* *Some possible answers:*
> *...feel or taste sounds / ...hear or taste shapes / ...tastes like pickles /*
> *...feels round / ...feels like a soft touch / ...L is black*

> **Optional Activity:** Collect some pictures from magazines to use as prompts for the students to make comments, using *look* + adjective. For example, a picture of a beach might produce *That looks great. It looks beautiful. It looks peaceful / quiet.* A picture of a busy city street might produce *It looks crowded. It looks noisy.*, etc.

c • Have students complete the conversations with the correct form of the verb. This could be done individually and then checked with a partner.

• Follow up by asking random students for their answers.

> *AK*
> 1b *I'm smelling* 1c *smell*
> 2a *sounds* 2b *He's practicing* 2c *think*
> 3a *seem* 3b *don't like* 3c *have* 3d *Are you looking*
> 4a *I'm doing* 4b *don't understand* 4c *Do you need*
> 5a *look* 5b *have* 5c *it's getting*

d • Look at the ideas and get one or two students to make true sentences.

• Give students time to think of and write down true sentences, using the suggestions in the boxes or their own ideas.

• Read the example sentences. Here are some more examples you could use: *You look tired. I feel really good today.* Have students work individually to write true sentences about themselves and people they know. Then have them compare sentences with a partner.

• Follow up by asking random pairs to share sentences with the whole class.

12 Speaking

a • Look at the questions. Read through and check understanding if necessary.

• Give students a short time to make notes of their own answers.

• Put students in pairs to interview each other and compare answers. Tell students they are going to present their partner's answers to a group, so they should make notes. Remind them that they should show interest (*Really? Why?*), agree or disagree (*So / Neither*), and express their own opinions (*I think / feel*).

b • Put students in small groups. Tell students to take turns presenting their partner's answers to the questions in 12a.

• Encourage other members of the group to make comments and ask follow-up questions as in 12a. They should have conversations, rather than just having individuals making short speeches.

• Follow up by asking each group to report any similarities or differences they discovered in their group.

13 ▶ Writing

a • Have students read the paragraph and answer the questions.

> **AK** *The writer's favorite smell is bread baking in the oven.*
> *The best friend's house smells wonderful. The baking bread makes the house seem warm and inviting.*

b • Tell students to write a paragraph describing one of their answers from section 12 in more detail. While they are writing, circulate and help when asked. If you read any of the writing before it's finished, comment on the content, not the language. Ask questions to help the student add more details.

> **Optional Activity:** Process writing. When students have finished, put them in pairs to read each other's paragraphs and make comments on the content. Encourage students to rewrite their paragraphs, including the details their partner asked for.
>
> When this is finished, students should look at the language. It's useful to do this in pairs, as it is often easier to spot another person's mistakes. They could help each other make corrections before posting the paragraphs for everyone to read.

c • Post the paragraphs around the classroom and have students circulate and read other students' paragraphs.

• Follow up by asking students to report on the different tastes, smells, sounds, and sights. Ask students which they thought was the most unusual.

• If you assign the writing for homework, do the pair work and exercise 13c in the next class.

3 Big screen, small screen

Main aims of this unit

Grammar: Present perfect simple + *still* / *yet* / *already*; obligation and permission: Modals and expressions

Vocabulary: Types of movies; adjectives with *-ed* / *-ing* endings

Functions: Asking for and giving opinions, agreeing and disagreeing

Unit Overview

Listening:	An interview with a filmmaker
Vocabulary:	Types of movies
Focus on Grammar:	Present perfect simple + *still* / *yet* / *already*
Speaking:	Taking a survey on movies
Language in Action:	Asking for and giving opinions, agreeing and disagreeing
Writing:	A movie review
KnowHow:	Building vocabulary
Listening:	An interview with an "extra" on a TV show
Vocabulary:	Adjectives with *-ed* / *-ing* endings
Focus on Grammar:	Obligation and permission: Modals and expressions
Reading:	The effects of TV watching
Speaking:	Comparing opinions about TV

Warm-up

Ask students if any of them have been to the movies recently. What movie did they see? Ask them if they read the credits (the list of names of people who worked in the movie).

1 ▶ Listening

a • Look at the movie credits. Ask students what they think each person does.

> **Pronunciation:** Cameron /ˈkæmərən/   Wyatt /ˈwaɪət/
> Adrienne /eɪdriˈɛn/   Hoopes /hups/
> Jaime /ˈdʒeɪmi/   Ike /aɪk/

> *AK* Director: *The person who instructs the actors, cameramen, and other people working on the movie.*
> Producer: *The person who has general control of the movie, especially of finances.*
> Editor: *The person who puts the "shots" of a movie together.*
> Casting director: *The person responsible for finding and contracting the actors.*

b • Look at the photographs. Tell students that Jennifer works in movies. Ask them what they think she does. Accept any suggestions. You could write their predictions on the board.

• Tell students they are going to listen to an interview with Jennifer. They should answer the questions *Which jobs has she done?* and *Which job would she like to do?* Tell them to look at the list of jobs in 1a to help.

• **AUDIO** Play the recording straight through. Ask students if their predictions were correct about what jobs Jennifer has done, and what she would like to do. If there is doubt or disagreement, play the recording again.

> *AK* She has written and directed a movie.
> She'd like to do more editing.

c • Read through the statements with the students. If any of the students think they know which statements are true or false, don't confirm their ideas. Ask them to listen and check.

• **AUDIO** Play the recording again for students to listen and mark the statements T (true) or F (false).

- **AUDIO** Play the recording again for students to check their answers. If there is doubt or disagreement, play the recording again, pausing after each item of information.

- Discuss the false statements with the whole class. Elicit the correct information from the students orally.

> **AK** 2 F *(It was hard to find time…)*
>   3 T
>   4 T
>   5 F *(She enjoyed shooting, even though it was tiring.)*
>   6 T

d • Either have a quick whole group discussion or put students in small groups to compare ideas about the questions.

2 ▸ Vocabulary: Types of movies

a • Look at the list of movie types. Read through with the students and check understanding if necessary. You could ask them to give examples of each type.

- Have students read the movie listings page and circle five more types of movies.

> **AK** *science fiction*   *comedy*   *documentary*
>   *animated movie*   *horror movie*

b • Tell students to make a list of the four types of movies they like best, in order of preference. Ask them to think of examples of each of their favorites.

- Put students in small groups to compare ideas. Remind them to use the plural when talking about things in general. For example, *My favorite movies are documentaries.*

- Follow up by asking each group to say which type of movie is the most popular in their group. Ask for some examples of movies for each type.

3 ▸ Focus on Grammar

a • Look at the chart. Have students identify the meanings of *still, yet, already*. If necessary, give them more examples, based on a personal situation. For example, *I haven't seen Lord of the Rings 3 yet. In fact, I still haven't seen Lord of the Rings 1. I've already seen…*

AK 1a *already*   1b *still, yet*
  2 Still *goes between the auxiliary and the main verb.*
    Yet *always goes at the end of the sentence.*
    Already *can go in either position.*

> **Language Note:** American English often uses the simple past with these adverbs. *I already did that. He didn't do it yet.* These adverbs also occur with other tenses. For example, *I'm still working at the same place. We're not living in our new house yet.*

b • Have students put the adverbs in the correct place in each sentence.

   AK 1 *...Joe* <u>still</u> *hasn't finished...*
      2 *...Sonia's* <u>already</u> *been... / ...Sonia's been in three movies* <u>already</u>.
      3 *...I* <u>still</u> *haven't had breakfast.*
      4 *I haven't seen the new one at the Lagoon Theater* <u>yet</u>.

   • Follow up orally, asking random students for their answers.

c • Read through the To Do list on Conrad's desk. Have students say what Conrad has or hasn't done. Point out the two ways of saying the same thing in the example.

   > **Pronunciation:** Lansing /ˈlænsɪŋ/   Ito /ˈitoʊ/

   AK *Some possible answers:*
      He has already called Lucy.
      He hasn't typed the ideas yet. OR *He still hasn't typed the ideas.*
      He has already bought the paint.
      He has already finished the letter.
      He still hasn't cleaned his desk. OR *He hasn't cleaned his desk yet.*

   • As a follow up, you could ask students to write sentences either in class or as homework.

d • Ask students to think back a few days and make a To Do list for this week. They should check the things they have done.

   • Put students in pairs to talk about the things they have done and the things they haven't done yet. Encourage the use of follow-up questions.

> **Optional Activity:** Set up this situation. The class is going to have a party to celebrate a special occasion or they're going on a trip. Put students into two groups and ask them to list the things they have done in order to prepare for the occasion. Then have groups take turns asking the other group *Have you ...yet?* If the item is on their list, they can answer *Yes, we've already done that* and score a point. If the item is **not** on their list, they must answer *No, we haven't done that yet.* In this case, the group asking the question scores a point.

4 Speaking

a • Tell students they are going to ask and answer the questions on the questionnaire. Put students in small groups and get them to make one answer sheet for the group. They shouldn't copy the questions, just the numbers. Have one student secretary make notes for the entire group.

• Have students ask the questions and record the answers for each student in the group.

b • Get groups to exchange answer sheets. Tell the groups to study the answers they have received and try to think of a movie to recommend for each person in the other group. They should write the names of the movies on the answer sheets.

• Follow up by returning the answer sheets to the original group. Have students look at the recommendations. Ask who liked the movie recommended for them.

> **Optional Activity:** Have students get into groups based on their favorite type of movie. Ask them to compare the movies they have already seen and those that they haven't seen yet. They ask *Have you seen...?* and other people in the group reply. If they have seen that particular movie, ask them to give their opinion of it.

5 Language in Action: Opinions

a • Ask students to cover the conversation and describe the picture.

• Books closed. Tell students they are going to listen to the conversation between Eddie and Maxine. They should answer the question *Do Eddie and Maxine have the same opinion about the movie?*

• **AUDIO** Play the recording straight through. Ask for the students' answers, and the reasons for them, but don't accept or reject any at this time.

- **AUDIO** Books open. Play the recording again. Tell students to listen and check their answer to the question. Follow up by asking students for their answer. Ask them why.

  > **AK** *They don't agree about this movie. (They agree that they like old-fashioned movies.)*

- **Help Desk:** Look at the expression and its meaning.

b • Read through the expressions in the chart with the students. Then tell them to complete the conversation in 5b with the expressions from the chart. They should choose an expression that makes sense in the context and not worry if they can't remember exactly what was said.

- **AUDIO** Play the recording again. Tell students to listen to see if they chose the same expression.

- Follow up by asking students to give their answers. Check what exactly was said and other possible expressions for each blank.

  > **AK** *(The first expression given is the one heard on the recording. Expressions in parentheses would also be appropriate in the situation.)*
  > *2 if you ask me (I think / In my opinion)*
  > *3 I don't think (I'm not sure)*
  > *4 maybe*
  > *5 I guess so (I suppose you're right)*
  > *6 I suppose you're right (I guess so / I agree)*

c • Put students in pairs to make conversations using the expressions from the chart. Tell them to try and keep the conversation going for more than just the two lines in the example.

- Circulate and listen. Follow up by asking a few pairs to repeat their conversation for the whole group.

6 ▶ Writing: A movie review

a • Look at the picture. Ask students where they think this article comes from: *A newspaper? A magazine?* Ask students if any of them know this classic movie. Ask them if they know what type of movie Alfred Hitchcock was famous for. Ask students if they think this is a contemporary review or from an old magazine.

> **In the Know:** Sir Alfred Hitchcock (1899–1980) was born in London and made movies in Britain and the United States. He was known as "the master of suspense." His other movies include *Psycho, The Birds,* and *Vertigo.*

- Tell students to read the review quickly and answer the question *What rating do you think the reviewer would give this movie?* Tell them not to worry about any words they don't know.

- Ask students for their answer. Ask them to give some of the words and phrases that helped them decide on a rating.

  AK *Possible answer:*
  ★★★★ *Excellent: "genuine classic"; "fascinating"; "unusual"; "stands out"; "the best"; "exceptional"; "superb"; "you won't be disappointed"*

> **In the Know:** *Rear Window* was remade in 1998 with Christopher Reeve playing the James Stewart part.

b - Tell students to read the review more slowly and underline the phrases that answer the questions. Follow up by asking random students for their answers.

  AK *Possible answers:*
  1 *a (tense) thriller*
  2 *Jeff, a photographer…; Grace Kelly…possible love interest; Jeff starts watching his neighbors…he notices some strange events…(believes) one of his neighbors is a murderer. Grace Kelly… helps him trap the killer.*
  3 *…most interesting aspects…is that the entire story takes place within Jeff's apartment…*
  4 *acting is exceptional and the directing is superb. …you won't be disappointed.*

c - Point out the use of the simple present to describe the events in the movie.

- Have students write a review of a movie they have seen, following the order of the questions in 6b. They should write one paragraph in answer to each question. Tell them to decide on a star rating for the movie but **not** to put it in their review.

d - Tell students to exchange reviews and decide what rating the writer would give the movie. Have students compare ratings.

- If you assign the writing as homework, do this in the next lesson.

7 *KnowHow*: Building vocabulary

a • Individually, have students look at the review in section 6 and find words and expressions used to describe the aspects of the movie.

> **AK** 2 *exceptional*
> 3 *fascinating and unusual viewpoint*
> 4 *stands out / superb*

b • Put students in pairs or groups. Tell them to compare their lists in **a** and to try to add more words to the lists.

c • Tell students to look at the review they wrote and add more words to make it even more descriptive.

Note: Process writing. Tell students that professional writers work with editors who ask questions and make suggestions to make the writing clearer or more interesting. When this has been done, a proofreader looks at the writing and corrects the language and punctuation. Tell them they are going to work as writers, editors, and proofreaders at different stages of this activity.

Professional writers not only work with editors, they also know who their "audience" is. Before students start writing, they should know what is going to happen to their paragraphs and who is going to read them.

Give students time to write their paragraphs. Then let students choose a partner to work with. They will be each other's editors. They should read each other's paragraphs and ask questions for clarification and more detail. They should look at the content of the paragraph.

Students should then rewrite their paragraphs, including the extra points and details.

Then tell students to act as proofreaders. They should exchange paragraphs again, look at the language, and make suggestions for corrections. If necessary, have students rewrite the paragraphs. The final versions of the paragraphs should be displayed, or "published" in order to make this work worthwhile.

8 Listening

a • Ask students how much television they watch. Do they watch more on the weekends? Ask them what types of TV shows they like or not like.

- List on the board the types of shows they mention. If they don't mention sitcoms, ask them about one that is on local TV. Try to get a good selection of types on the board.

> AK *Possible types of shows:*
> *news / sitcom / talk show / drama / game show / soap opera / sports*

In the Know: A *sitcom* is a situational comedy.

- Ask students to give examples of the different types of shows from local TV. Either have a quick class discussion about the types of shows the students watch or ask them to compare what they watch with a partner.

b • Tell students they are going to listen to Charlie talking about being an "extra" on a TV show.

- Get students to discuss their answers to questions 1 and 2 in pairs. Follow up by asking pairs for their predictions. OR Brainstorm guesses and write them on the board.

- **AUDIO** Play the recording straight through. Tell students to listen and check their guesses.

> AK *Possible answers:*
> 1 *An "extra" is a background person who has no real role in a show. The "extra" may, for example, walk down a street, sit at a table in a restaurant scene, or stand around in a party scene.*
> 2 *No, they don't. Sometimes "extras" have to pretend to speak.*

c • Read through the unfinished sentences in the exercise. If any of the students can finish them from memory, don't confirm their ideas but tell them to write notes and listen again to check.

- **AUDIO** Play the recording again. Tell students to make notes to finish the sentences. Tell them to write only one or two words to help them remember the information, not to try to write everything while they're listening.

- Give students time to complete the sentences from their notes.

- **AUDIO** Follow up by playing the recording again, pausing at relevant points, and checking answers with the students. Check that they have the correct information—it's not necessary for them to repeat the exact words.

AK 1 *...there's a lot of waiting around.*
    2 *...you're doing a scene.*
    3 *...two...*
    4 *...stand or walk around.*
    5 *...he looked like him.*
    6 *...sitcom.*

d • Either have a whole class discussion or put students in small groups to answer the questions.

9 Vocabulary: Adjectives with *-ed* / *-ing* endings

a • Have students look at the example sentences 1 and 2 and answer the questions.

AK The -ed *form* confused *describes how the person feels.*
    The -ing *form* confusing *describes the movie that makes him feel that way.*

b • Look at the picture and the caption. Ask *How does the man feel?* (*Frustrated.*) *What's the crossword puzzle like?* (*Frustrating.*)

• Read through the word list. Have students fill in the blanks with the correct form of an adjective from the list. Tell them that, in some cases, more than one adjective is possible.

AK 2 *tired*
    3 *disappointing* OR *frustrating*
    4 *disappointing* OR *boring* OR *confusing* OR *frustrating*
    5 *disappointed* OR *frustrated* OR *confused* OR *surprised*
    6 *confusing* OR *frustrating*

c • Give students a moment to think about the examples. Then put students in pairs to talk about the ideas suggested in items 1 and 2.

• Suggest that students write some of these sentences in their notebooks to help them remember the difference between *-ing* and *-ed* adjectives.

10 Focus on Grammar

a • Have students look at the chart and answer the questions.

AK 1 *need to, have to, must*
    2 *are / aren't allowed to*
    3 *must*

Language Note: The expression *need to* is not as strong as *have to*. *Have to* sounds authoritarian and commanding. *Must* indicates the strongest necessity and displays strong emotion.

b • Have students read the notice. Explain that these are instructions to extras in a TV show.

• Look at the correction in the first sentence. Tell students there are five more mistakes that they should correct. This could be done individually or in pairs.

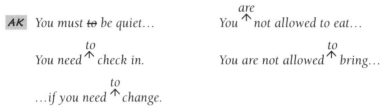

> *AK*   *You must ~~to~~ be quiet...*   *You ^are not allowed to eat...*
>
> *You need ^to check in.*   *You are not allowed ^to bring...*
>
> *...if you need ^to change.*

c • Put students in pairs to practice expressions of obligation and permission.

• Remind them to keep the conversations going by agreeing (*so / neither*) or asking follow-up questions.

Optional Activity: Set up this situation. Foreigners are coming to visit your country and need some information about laws and customs. Have groups of students prepare a helpful list to be given to tourists at the airport or in hotels. Students should use expressions of obligation and permission. Encourage students to give reasons where appropriate.

11 ▷ Reading

a • Put students in small groups to discuss questions 1 and 2. Follow up by asking groups for their main ideas.

• Write some of the students' ideas on the board and leave them there to refer to later in the discussion in 11e.

b • Tell students to read the two articles quickly. Ask *What do the articles say about the questions in 11a?* Ask random students for their answers.

> *AK*   *Possible answers:*
> 1 *People felt relaxed and passive.*
> 2 *People are getting smarter (IQ scores are rising), and this may be because of TV and video games.*

> **Pronunciation:** irony /'aɪrəni/
> Ulric Neisser /ˌʌlrɪk 'naɪzər/
> theory /'θiəri/

> **Optional Activity:** Jigsaw reading. Divide the class into two groups. Group A, read article A and Group B, read article B. Then make pairs, one student from group A and one from group B to answer the questions in 11a. In 11c the group A students read article B and answer the questions (5–7), and the group B students read article A and answer the questions (1–4). Have students form the same pairs and exchange answers, so that, in the end, they have all read both articles and have the answers to all the questions.

c • Have students read the articles again to decide if statements 1–7 are true or false. Follow up by asking random students for their answers.

> **AK** 1 *False. Two out of five adults and seven out of ten teenagers…*
> 2 *True.*
> 3 *False. Participants…reported that TV took away their energy.*
> 4 *True.*
> 5 *False. …IQs around the world have gone up steadily.*
> 6 *True.*
> 7 *False. The most improvement has been in solving visual problems and answering questions creatively.*

d • This exercise could be done in pairs or done individually and compared with a partner. Ask students to find the words or expressions in the articles and match them to the definitions.

> **AK** 1 *passive*   2 *concentrating*
> 3 *mood*   4 *a great deal of*
> 5 *steadily*   6 *rewarding*

e • Summarize the activity by asking students if what they have learned from the articles has changed the answers they gave in 11a.

• Refer students back to the ideas you recorded on the board in 11a.

12 Speaking

a • Ask students to read the statements and circle the number that indicates how much they agree or disagree with each one. Give them a few minutes to do this.

b • Put students in pairs or small groups to compare their opinions. Make sure they give reasons for their opinions and that they keep the conversation going with follow-up questions.

c • Put students in groups to make a summary statement about TV that they all agree on. Remind them about the language of agreeing and disagreeing in section 5.

• A group statement might contain statements like these: *TV can be a useful way to learn about the world. But some TV shows are too violent.*

> **Optional Activity:** You could summarize this part of the unit by making a poster with the groups' statements in a spidergram around the subject of TV.

Units 1–3 Review

Grammar

1 *Possible answer:*
Katie is a casting director. Her job is difficult, but she loves it.
She gets frustrated sometimes, but her job is very satisfying.

2 2 *did I*   3 *did I*   4 *am I*

3 2 *working*   3 *losing*   4 *to talk*   5 *to call*   6 *to see*

4 1 *are working*   2 *is looking*   3 *look*   4 *thinks*
5 *does not (doesn't) sound*   6 *is ('s) thinking*   7 *do not (don't) have*

5 2 *have not (haven't) called her yet*   3 *have ('ve) already talked*
4 *still have not (haven't) heard from*   5 *have ('ve) already talked to her*

6 2 *are not (aren't) allowed to*
3 *were allowed to*
4 *were not (weren't) allowed to*

7 *Answers will vary.*

Vocabulary

8 1 *chores*   2 *documentary*   3 *fascinating*
4 *get better*   5 *celebration*   6 *sweep*

Recycling Center

9 long   <u>*longer*</u>   longest
big   bigger   <u>*biggest*</u>
good   <u>*better*</u>   <u>*best*</u>
hard   <u>*harder*</u>   <u>*hardest*</u>
bad   <u>*worse*</u>   <u>*worst*</u>
difficult   more difficult   <u>*most difficult*</u>

10 1 *hardest*   2 *more complicated*   3 *worst*
4 *harder*   5 *simpler*   6 *more difficult*

Fun Spot

Some possible answers:
two-letter words: an, as, at, he, hi, in, it
three-letter words: ate, eat, eye, hat, his, sat, say, set, sit, ten, the, yes
four-letter words: easy, neat, sent, stay, than, then, thin, this
five-letter words: sheet, shine

4 In the mind's eye

Main aims of this unit

Grammar: Past continuous; comparatives: Review and extension

Vocabulary: Common expressions with *come* and *go*; compound adjectives

Functions: Trying to remember

Unit Overview

Listening:	Looking at photographs
Vocabulary:	Common expressions with *come* and *go*
Focus on Grammar:	Past continuous
Speaking:	Describing your earliest memory
Reading:	A Memory Artist
Writing:	Describing a place from memory
Focus on Grammar:	Comparatives: Review and extension
Listening:	Tatiana Cooley: A memory champion
Vocabulary:	Compound adjectives
Language in Action:	Trying to remember
KnowHow:	Sentence stress (unstressed words)
Reading and Speaking:	Memory techniques

Warm-up

Ask students *Do you have a good memory? What kind of things do you find difficult to remember? What do you find easy to remember?*

1 ▶ Listening

a • Have students describe the photos, saying what is happening in each one.

> **AK** *Possible answers:*
> A *Some people are skiing /'skiɪŋ/. Maybe they are at a ski resort.*
> B *Some people are at a party in a private home.*
> C *Two men are carrying furniture into an apartment. Maybe someone is moving in.*

b • **AUDIO** Tell students that they are going to listen to Kristy and Hugh talk about events that they remember. Play the recording straight through. Students should listen to the conversation and write the letters of the photos in the order Kristy and Hugh talk about them. Tell them not to worry about details of the conversations at this time.

• **AUDIO** Check the order with the students. If there is any doubt or disagreement, play the recording again, pausing after each section. Get students to say which words helped them with their answers.

> **AK** *The correct order is B, C, A*

c • Read through the statements with the students. Ask students to mark any of them that they think they know and listen to check these and complete the others.

• **AUDIO** Play the recording again. Check answers following the same procedure as in 1b. Ask students for the reasons for their answers.

> **AK** 1 F (*He doesn't remember coming back early.*)
> 2 F (*He came back early.*)
> 3 T (*Who's that? It's Kenny.*)
> 4 F (*They finally did it, but it took ages.*)
> 5 T
> 6 F (*She fell and hurt her ankle.*)

d • Either have a quick class discussion or put students in pairs to talk about whether they like looking at photos from different times. Ask if students have any photos that bring back special memories.

> **Optional Activity:** Ask students to bring some personal photos to the next class. Put them in pairs to ask and answer about the photos, as in the conversation here.

2 Vocabulary: Common expressions with *come* and *go*

a • Have students read the sentences and match the expressions with their meanings. Most of the expressions are in the listening in section 1. If necessary, students could look at the audioscript to get more context for these sentences.

• This exercise could be done in pairs or individually and checked with a partner. Follow up by asking random students for their answers.

> **AK** 1 *h*   2 *e*   3 *g*   4 *d*   5 *f*   6 *a*   7 *b*

• **Help Desk:** Read through the explanation of *come* and *go* with the students. Ask them to give more examples. If they have any difficulty, follow one or both of these suggestions:

1 Tell a student *Come here.* Then say *Go to the door.* Use gestures to reinforce the direction of the movement.

2 Give more examples: *I waited outside when my friend went in to see the doctor. I was in my office when the boss came in.*

b • Have students fill in the blanks with the correct forms of expressions with *come* or *go*. Remind them to be careful with the verb forms.

• Follow up by asking random students for their answers.

> **AK** 2 *Come in*
> 3 *went away*
> 4 *come over*
> 5 *come back*
> 6 *go out*

3 Focus on Grammar

a • Have students look at the chart and answer the questions.

> **AK** 1 *past continuous*
> 2 *simple past*
> 3 was / were + -ing *form of the verb*

> **Language Note:** *When* and *while* connect two activities happening at the same time. *When* usually introduces a time clause in which an action has happened or will happen once. *While* usually introduces a time clause with a continuing (lasting) action. *While* often emphasizes that two activities are simultaneous.

b • Look at the example in the exercise. You could mime the action (*leaving the office*) and then make the sound of the phone to help students see the difference in the timing of the actions.

• Have students fill in the blanks with the past continuous or simple past. This could be done in pairs or individually and then checked with a partner.

> **AK** 2 *started / were playing*
> 3 *was waiting / arrived*
> 4 *broke / was driving*
> 5 *came / were talking*
> 6 *saw / was walking*

c • Read the complete paragraph with the students without saying which verb tense is correct. For example, you could just say "ba-ba-ba" for each verb, but make sure the students understand the gist of the story before they start to choose the correct verb forms.

• Have students choose the correct form of the verbs.

> **AK** 2 *was raining*   3 *were riding*   4 *wanted*   5 *was turning*
> 6 *ran*   7 *fell*   8 *broke*   9 *was walking*
> 10 *hurt*   11 *didn't break*

d • Give students a short time to think of (or, if necessary, invent) something that happened to them.

• Put students in pairs or small groups to describe the event. Remind the listeners to comment and ask follow-up questions.

• Circulate and listen. The students' performance in this task will show you if they need more practice.

Optional Activities: (a) Collect some pictures from magazines that have people doing things (riding bikes, watching TV, etc.). Set up a situation. For example, say *Last Sunday there was a terrible storm. It started raining at four o'clock.* Ask *What were these people doing when it started to rain?* You could then ask *What do you think they did next?*

(b) Create practice cards by mounting a picture of a person (or people) doing something on one side of a piece of cardboard and a picture of a different event or activity on the other side. For example, on one side of the card there might be a picture of a man walking in the park, and on the other side a picture of a rainy day. Students make sentences using both pictures. For example, *He was walking in the park when it started to rain.* If you show the rainy side first, students should make the sentence in a different order. *It was raining when he went for a walk in the park.*

(c) A few minutes after the beginning of a class, ask students *What were you doing when I came in?*

4 Speaking

a • Tell students they are going to talk about their earliest memory. Read the questions and ask students to take a minute or two to just think about them to see how much they can remember.

b • Put students in small groups to describe their earliest memory and discuss the questions. Remind students to ask questions for more detail.

• Follow up by asking each group to report to the class.

5 Reading

a • Ask students to describe the pictures. What differences or similarities can they find?

> **Pronunciation:** Magnani /mɑnˈyɑni/   Pontito /poʊnˈtitoʊ/

b • Have students read the article and note what they find surprising.

> *AK* Possible answers:
> *He paints from memory.*
> *He is self-taught.*
> *Each painting begins from a memory flash.*

c • You could get students to do this exercise from memory first and then read the article again to check. Follow up by asking random students for their answers and for the words or phrases that helped them decide.

>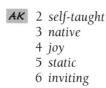
>
> 1 T
> 2 F *(Until recently he had not even seen a photograph…)*
> 3 NI
> 4 T
> 5 T
> 6 F *(He feels urgency…onto paper immediately.)*
> 7 F *(…not static like a photograph…he can look around.)*
> 8 NI

d • Students could do this exercise in pairs. Point out that the numbers refer to the paragraph that includes the word.

> AK 2 *self-taught*
> 3 *native*
> 4 *joy*
> 5 *static*
> 6 *inviting*

e • Either have a class discussion or put students in small groups to express their ideas.

6 ▶ Writing

a • Look at the picture and read through the example paragraph with the students.

• Give students time to think about a place from their past. You could ask them to close their eyes. Then ask some questions. For example, *What kind of place is it? A house, a garden, in a city, in the country, where? What colors can you remember? Are they bright colors? What do you remember doing there? Who do you remember there? Is it anybody special? etc.* Ask the questions in a quiet, calm voice.

• Have students write their paragraphs in class or assign the writing for homework.

b • Put students in pairs to read and listen to their paragraphs. They should ask their partner at least two questions about what they wrote. Possible questions: *Have you returned to this place…?, Why do you think you remember it so well?*

Note: Explain that questions could be of two types:

1 Detail-oriented questions to encourage the writer to elaborate on description. For example, *How old were you when you went to…?*

2 General interest questions about the place and any people related to it, for example, *How big was the garden? Did your grandfather grow other things?*

- When the writing is finished, display the paragraphs on the wall as a poster, or in a class book.

> **Optional Activity:** After students have discussed the content of the paragraphs, have them look at the language and help each other correct any grammar mistakes, join sentences together to make more complex structures, or rephrase sentences to make the meaning clearer.

7 Focus on Grammar

a • Read through the sentences in the chart while students are looking at the pictures. Then ask questions 1–3.

> **AK** 1 *Use -er with one-syllable adjectives; use* more *and* less *with most adjectives with two or more syllables.*
> 2 *Use* as…as.
> 3 *It means* less.

Note: For two-syllable adjectives that end in -y change the -y to i, for example, *prettier, sillier,* and *chillier.*

b • Read the example with the students. Have students write their sentences. Follow up by asking random students for their answers.

> **AK** 2 *The painting of the house is <u>less beautiful than</u> the outdoor scene.*
> 3 *The painting is <u>as pretty as</u> the photograph.* OR *The photograph is <u>as pretty as</u> the painting.*
> 4 *The photograph is <u>not as interesting as</u> the painting.*
> 5 *The paintings are <u>more expensive than</u> these photographs.*

c • Have students look at the two pictures of the same place at different time periods. Work with the students to write one sentence comparing the two places as an example.

- Have students write as many sentences as they can comparing the two pictures, using the structures given.

- This exercise could be done individually or in pairs with the students if necessary. Remind students that they will need to use the past tense in some of their sentences.

- Follow up by asking random students for their sentences.

> **Optional Activity:** This is an opportunity for students to express their own ideas. Ask students to choose a topic. For example, clothes, hairstyles, technology, etc. Write at least five sentences about how things have changed in the past five years. Put students in pairs to talk about what they wrote. Ask them to close their notebooks for this, so that they don't just read out their sentences. Encourage the listener to make comments and ask follow-up questions. Circulate and listen. The students' performance in this activity will show you if they need to practice more.

8 ▶ Listening

a • Look at the list of words and their definitions. Have students match the words and their definitions. This exercise could be done in pairs.

- Follow up by asking random students for their answers.

- **AUDIO** Play the recording for students to check their answers.

  AK 2 *a*   3 *b*   4 *e*   5 *c*

b • Have a quick class discussion. Note some of the students' ideas on the board and keep them there to refer to later in the activity.

c • Tell students they are going to listen to part of a radio program about a memory champion, Tatiana Cooley.

- **AUDIO** Play the recording straight through. Students should listen for two reasons that Tatiana's memory is special or unusual.

  AK *Possible answers:*
  She can remember large numbers of things like names, faces, poems, and numbers. She's incredibly absent-minded! (She can't remember if she has six or seven brothers and sisters.)

> **Language Note:** On the recording about Tatiana Cooley, the reporter says, "...when ask<u>ed</u> how many brothers and sisters she <u>has</u>, she repli<u>ed</u>...." This use of indirect speech with *asked* followed by a present tense verb (*has*) is idiomatic. It is justifiable because it is referring to a general situation, not an action. It's also true that in conversation people don't always follow the strict rules for sequence of tenses.

d • Read through the sentences. If students can do any of them from memory, don't confirm their answers. Ask them to listen and check.

• **AUDIO** Play the recording straight through again for students to listen and circle the correct answers.

• **AUDIO** Follow up by playing the recording and pausing after each piece of information is given and checking with the students.

AK   1 *70 of 100*   2 *six or seven*
      3 *different processes*   4 *anyone*
      5 *two*   6 *in college*

• Check back with the notes from the discussion in 8b. Are there similarities between students' ideas about memory and Tatiana Cooley's?

e • If you have time, this exercise could be extended into a short discussion. Put students in small groups to discuss the question and give reasons. They could also give examples of their own memory or absent-mindedness, exchange ideas on techniques they use to remember or memorize things, and talk about the kind of things they try to memorize and why.

• Follow up by asking groups for the most interesting thing they learned about a classmate.

9 ▶ Vocabulary: Compound adjectives

a • Explain that a compound adjective is an adjective made up of two (or more) words, usually joined by a hyphen.

> **Language Note:** The use of hyphens in English is very complicated. If your students ask, tell them the best solution is to look in a dictionary if they're not sure.

• Have students read the paragraph and underline the compound adjectives. Follow up by checking that students understand the meaning of the adjectives.

AK   *well-known: (famous)*
      absent-minded: (forgets things easily)
      To Do: (a list of things to do)
      full-time: (all day, every day)
      brand-new: (completely new; not second-hand)
      well-dressed: (wears nice clothes)
      left-handed / right-handed: (uses the left / right hand to write)

> **Language Note:** If students ask, the adjective for someone who uses both hands equally is *ambidextrous.*

b • Check that students understand the meaning of the adjectives on the list. They should be able to work them out for themselves.

• Have students fill in the blanks with an adjective from the list.

> **AK** 2 *good-looking*
> 3 *right-handed*
> 4 *full-time*

c • Look at the example and then give students a few minutes to write five sentences about themselves or people or things they know.

• Follow up by asking random students to read out their best sentence.

10 Language in Action: Trying to remember

a • Tell students that the two people in the picture are trying to remember something.

• **AUDIO** Tell students to listen and answer the questions *What are they trying to remember?* and *Do they remember it?* Play the recording straight through.

• Check the responses with the whole class.

> **AK** *They are trying to remember the name of an (Italian) restaurant. No, they don't remember it.*

b • **AUDIO** Give students time to read the expressions in the box. Then have them listen again and mark the expressions they hear. Play the recording straight through.

• **AUDIO** Follow up by playing the recording again, pausing after each expression to check the answers.

> **AK** ✓ *I can't remember.*
> ✓ *I can't think of it.*
> ✓ *It's on the tip of my tongue.*
> ✓ *It'll come to me in a minute.*
> ✓ *Remind me to…*

c • Put students in pairs to make conversations about trying to remember.

• You may need to practice the pronunciation of *It's on the tip of my tongue* and *I'll think of it in a minute* before they start.

• Circulate and listen. Follow up by asking random pairs to present their conversation to the group.

11 ▸ *KnowHow*: Sentence stress (unstressed words)

a • **AUDIO** Tell students to read the sentence silently to themselves. Play the recording for students and tell them to underline the unstressed words.

> **AK** It's <u>on</u> <u>the</u> tip <u>of</u> <u>my</u> tongue.

Note: The words with primary stress—*tip* and *tongue*—are marked with medium black dots. *It's* has a secondary stress and is marked with a smaller dot.

• Ask students *Are the unstressed words information words or grammar words? (Grammar words.)*

b • Have students mark the stressed words or syllables in sentences 1–3 and then practice saying them.

c • **AUDIO** Play the recording for the students to check their responses to 11b.

> **AK** 1 It'll come to me in a second.
>
>   2 I'll think of it in a minute.
>
>   3 This one's better than that one.

• Have students practice saying the sentences with the correct stress. You could tap out the rhythm of the sentence or clap your hands on the stressed words. Ask *Why are the demonstrative words* this *and* that *stressed in sentence 3? (Because the speaker is emphasizing the contrast between two things.)*

• ***Help Desk:*** Point out that the information words are usually stressed because they carry the main ideas of the sentence. However, this can make it difficult, especially for non-native speakers, to understand the other words in the sentence. Compare the stress patterns with the students' own language.

12 ▸ Reading and Speaking

a • Have students read the first article carefully and follow the instructions for contrasting the two methods of remembering the list. Follow up by asking if they found the "trip technique" helpful.

- **Option:** Have students work in pairs. Tell students to write two "shopping lists" of 10 items for their partner to memorize. With the first list they try to memorize it by just looking at it for one minute, without using the "trip technique." They then return the list to their partner and write down as many items as they can. With the second list they also take one minute, but as they are looking at the list, they use the "trip technique" described in the article. They return the list to their partner and then write as many items as they can remember, thinking about their "trip."

As a follow up to this activity, compile a chart for the class with the scores to determine which system enabled students to remember more items.

- Have students read the second article and time themselves as they answer the two sets of questions. Ask if they were quicker on set one or set two.

- Ask for the words they thought of. If they have not managed to think of answers, use the examples below.

  > **AK** *Possible answers:*
  > Set 1: *lemon, cat, France, peas*
  > Set 2: *peach, elephant, Germany, carrot*

b • Ask the question. Have a quick class discussion.

c • Give students time to complete the chart.

- Put students in small groups to compare answers and discuss techniques they use or will try out in the future. Follow up by asking groups for their most useful techniques.

- The following are some suggestions of techniques. (a) for new vocabulary: recording the words in topic groups with drawings, translations, or true example sentences. (b) irregular verbs: memorizing true or nonsense sentences with the irregular verbs in them, associating irregular verb forms with other similar words, for example, *I've been eating beans.*

> **Optional Activity:** To round off this unit, the students could make a spidergram with the word *remember* in the center and suggestions of all the techniques they could use to help improve their ability to remember things.

5 Stuff of life

Main aims of this unit

Grammar: Relative clauses (subject); structures with phrasal verbs: Word order

Vocabulary: Adjectives for materials; parts of things and how things work

Functions: What's it called?

Warm-up

Ask students if any of them play guitar and what kind of music they play. Ask them how many famous guitarists they can think of.

In the Know: Many guitars are played with a *pick*. A pick is a small piece of plastic you use to pluck the strings of guitars. Some guitars are made with pickguards to prevent damage when using a pick. Willie Nelson's guitar "Trigger" was designed without a pickguard. Since Nelson plays "Trigger" with a pick anyway, a large hole has formed in the front of it.

1 ▷ Reading

a • Look at the picture. Have students describe it and answer the questions. Don't worry if they don't recognize the person, as there is information about him in the article.

b • Tell students to read the article but not to worry about words they don't know at this point.

 • Have students read the article quickly and choose the best summary. Follow up by asking students for their answer and why they chose it.

   AK 3

c • Have students read the article again more slowly and answer the questions. They could compare their answers with a partner.

 • Follow up by asking random students for their answers and the reasons for them.

   AK 1 *Nelson got Trigger in 1969.*
   2 *It has a hole on the front. It has signatures scratched into it.*
   3 *He is sentimental about the hole.*
   4 *Nelson's old guitar got broken, so he sent it to a friend for repair. His friend couldn't fix it, so he sold him a classical guitar he had for $750.*

 • Deal with any vocabulary problems now. Words and phrases you could highlight are *nickname(d)* (par. 1), *worn, weathered, sentimental* (par. 2), *autographed, scratched* (par. 3), *off the shelf* (par. 4).

> **In the Know:** Willie Nelson is a country and western singer, songwriter, and guitarist. He was born in Abbot, Texas. He had many country music hits in the 1960s. He has recorded over 100 albums.

d • Go over this list of items with the whole class. Mention some examples of buildings (houses, office buildings, museums) or household appliances (refrigerators, can openers, stoves) where people might prefer old or new ones for different reasons.

• Either have a whole class discussion or put students in small groups.

• If the students worked in groups, follow up by asking the groups for a majority opinion on each topic.

2 Focus on Grammar

a • Have students look at the chart and match the words to their use.

> **AK**   1 *who: B*   2 *which: C*   3 *that: A*

• **Help Desk:** Read through with the students. Ask if this is different in their language. See the Language Note below.

> **Language Note:** This section presents only relative clauses in which the relative pronoun (*who, which,* or *that*) is the subject of the clause. In English the relative pronoun cannot be omitted when it is the subject of the clause. Omitting it would result in a sentence like *He is a musician plays country music,* which is incorrect.
>
> It is not necessary to explain this to the students unless they ask or you think that it would help them understand this point in the Help Desk. Relative clauses with the relative pronoun as object will be presented in Student Book 3 of this series.

b • Read the example with the students. Point out that the relative pronoun (*who* or *that*) replaces the subject of the second sentence.

• Ask students to rewrite the sentences using relative pronouns. Point out that there are two correct answers for two items (#1 and #5).

> **AK**   1 OR *Nicole Shelby is a musician that plays jazz music.*
>   2 *She has made two CDs that have won awards.*
>   3 *She often plays in a club that has live music every night.*
>   4 *Nicole and her husband live in a house that has two pianos in it.*
>   5 *They have a son who is two years old.* OR *They have a son that is two years old.*

c • Give students time to write their definitions.

• Either put students in pairs to read their definitions and guess what the words are, or get them to circulate and read each definition to a different student.

> **Optional Activity:** Put the class into small groups and ask them to prepare five questions to ask another group. Give them these models for their questions: *What's the word for a person who (drives a bus)?* OR *What's the word for a thing that (you wear on your head on hot days)?* Then ask one person from each group to move around to another group and ask the questions. If you have time and the students are enjoying the activity, the questioners could move on again. This can also be played as a team game, with the teams asking and answering all of each other's questions.

3 Vocabulary: Adjectives for materials

a • Look at the pictures and the captions. Have students complete the blanks with *glass / wooden / metal*.

• **AUDIO** Play the recording for them to check their answers.

> **AK** a <u>wooden</u> guitar
> a <u>glass</u> window
> a <u>metal</u> clothes hanger

b • Give students a short time to make their lists. Compare answers in pairs or small groups.

• Follow up by asking random students for examples.

4 Listening

a • Look at the pictures and have students describe each item. Encourage them to use the vocabulary for materials.

• Put students in pairs to compare their ideas about which thing is important to which person(s). Tell students to give reasons for their ideas.

• Ask pairs to report their guesses. Write the names of the people in the exercise (*Mauricio, Elaine,…*) on the board and after each name write the object(s) students think are important to them.

b • **AUDIO** Play the recording for students to check their predictions.

AK   Mauricio: *motorcycle and backpack*
Elaine: *ring*
Lars and Ruth: *basket of family memories*
Bruce: *stereo and CDs*
Mia: *watch*

c • Tell students they are going to listen again and that they should make notes of one thing they hear about each object: what it's used for, where it came from, or any other information.

• **AUDIO** Play the recording again and pause briefly after each speaker to give students time to make notes. They shouldn't try to write complete sentences.

• Put students in pairs to compare their answers. Follow up by asking random students for the extra information they heard about each item.

AK   *Possible answers:*
1 *grandmother's, favorite possession, beautiful, gold, diamond, really special*
2 *go to work, carry everything I need*
3 *photographs, letters, pictures, art that our children made, family history*
4 *save a long time, at least 100 CDs, music from around the world*
5 *mother's watch, isn't expensive, old-fashioned, gold, leather band*

5 Speaking

a • Put students in small groups. Make sure they make one chart of favorite or important things for the group.

• Encourage the listeners to make comments and ask follow-up questions.

b • Ask each group to suggest the item from their group that is the oldest and compare with the other groups. Repeat for the most practical and the most unusual.

6 Language in Action: What's it called?

a • Look at the picture. Have students predict what they think the girl is trying to do.

• **AUDIO** Tell students to cover the conversation on the page. Play the recording straight through. Ask students what Lily is trying to do.

AK   *Fix a picture frame.*

b • Have students read the conversation and complete it with expressions from the chart.

• **AUDIO** Play the recording again for students to check their answers.

> **AK** 1 *it's like…*
> 2 *You use it to…*
> 3 *I'm not sure what it's called.*
> 4 *It looks like…*

• **Help Desk:** Read through with the students. Ask students for some examples or give some examples yourself. For example, *You use a pen for writing / to write letters. You use a pan to cook / for cooking.* You could also start the examples and have students complete them. For example, T: *You use a toothbrush…* Ss: *to brush / for brushing your teeth.* T: *You use a computer to…* Ss: *write e-mail / play games.* T: *You use a broom for…* Ss: *sweeping the floor.*

c • Put students in pairs to make conversations about the objects in the pictures.

> **Language Note:** A *paring knife* is a small knife used for peeling fruit and vegetables. The word *scissors* is always plural. To count scissors, say *a pair of scissors, three pairs of scissors.*

7 ▶ *KnowHow*: When you don't know a word

a • Have students look at the strategies in the chart.

• Have a quick class discussion on which ones they have used. Point out that there are probably times when they need a word they don't know in their own language. Can they relate any stories about times when this has happened to them? What was the word and what did they do?

b • Put students in pairs to practice using at least three of the strategies.

• Follow up by asking some pairs to repeat one of their conversations for the whole group. See if anyone can give the name of the object.

> **Optional Activity:** Ask students to bring mystery objects to class, for example, an unusual tool of some kind or something that is part of an object. They should show the object to the class for the other students to guess what it is. For example, *I think it's a…. It's used for….* The wilder the guesses the more amusing this activity can be.

8 ▶ Listening

a • Look at the pictures. Either have a class discussion or put students in pairs or small groups to discuss the questions.

  • Follow up with a show of hands for each item to find out which items students use most and least often, which they think are most difficult to operate, and which are easiest.

b • Tell students that they are going to listen to a conversation about one of the objects in 8a. They should listen and answer the questions *Which object are they talking about?* and *What's the problem?*

  • **AUDIO** Play the recording straight through. Ask students for their answers. If there is any doubt or disagreement, play the recording again.

  > **AK** 1 *The toaster oven.*
  > 2 *He can't operate the toaster oven. (He says that it drives me crazy…it doesn't do what I expect it to.)*

c • Read through the list with the students. Check that students understand the words *dial* (the instrument, usually round, which shows the options of temperature) and *button* (a small control which you push to start or stop a machine).

  • **AUDIO** Tell students to listen again and write Y (*Yes*) or N (*No*) in the blanks. Play the recording again straight through. Follow up by asking random students for their answers. If there is disagreement, play the recording again, pausing at appropriate points for the students to check.

  > **AK** 1 Y   2 Y   3 N   4 N   5 Y   6 N   7 Y   8 N

9 ▶ Vocabulary: Parts of things and how things work

a • Have students look at the diagram and put words from the diagram in the blanks in the instructions.

  > **AK** *handle   on / off button   temperature dial*

b • Put students in pairs to take turns role-playing the situation with the different objects. Tell the listener to ask questions to help.

  • Follow up by asking one or two pairs to present one of their conversations to the whole group.

10 ▶ Focus on Grammar

a • Read through the note on phrasal verbs with the students. Have students look at the chart and answer the question *Which type of word cannot go after the second word in the phrasal verb?*

> **AK**   *Object pronoun.*

> **Language Note:** Some phrasal verbs are separable, which means that an object can be placed between the two words in the phrasal verb. For example, *He **picked** the shirt **up**.* Other phrasal verbs are inseparable, which means that an object cannot come between the two words in the phrasal verb. For example, *Let's **go over** the test.* NOT ~~Let's go the test over.~~ Unfortunately, there is no general rule to know if a phrasal verb can be separated or not.

b • Have students read the definitions of verbs 1–5 and then look at exercise 8c to find more phrasal verbs to fill in the blanks in items 6–9.

> **AK**   6 *turn up*   7 *turn down*   8 *turn off*   9 *throw away*

> **Language Note:** With appliances like refrigerators or air conditioners, whose purpose is to cool things, *turn up* and *turn down* have the opposite meaning when referring to temperature. When you *turn up* the air conditioner, the air becomes colder. When you *turn it down*, it is less cold.

c • Read the example with the students. Point out that both forms are correct, because *the TV* is not an object pronoun. However, they only need to use one form in their answers.

• Have students complete the blanks with phrasal verbs and the objects in parentheses. They could compare their answers with a partner before the follow up.

• Follow up by asking random students for the complete sentence. Ask another student to give the alternative answer where appropriate.

> **AK**   2 *...turn the oven off...* OR *...turn off the oven...*
> 3 *...put them down...*
> 4 *...turn the lights on...* OR *...turn on the lights...*
> 5 *...put it away*
> 6 *...pick them up*

d • Have students answer the questions in complete sentences.

> **AK**   *Answers will vary.*

- Suggest that students reserve a page in their notebooks for phrasal verbs. They could start by writing their answers to this section to show the meaning of the phrasal verbs. They could add more personal sentences to show the meaning of other phrasal verbs.

11 ▶ Speaking

a • Give students time to complete the statements with their own words. Then have them compare answers with a partner.

b • Put students in groups to compare and discuss their statements. Encourage comments and follow-up questions.

- Get each group to decide what they think is the most and least useful invention of the last hundred years.

- Follow up by asking each group for their suggestions and have a quick class discussion to try to agree. You could ask students to vote on the most useful item.

12 ▶ Reading

a • Look at the pictures and get students to speculate about what they are.

- Tell students to read the article quickly without worrying about new vocabulary. They should answer the questions and check if their ideas about the pictures were correct. Follow up orally.

  AK 1 *Answers will vary. Accept any reasonable response. They are designed to solve everyday problems, but they also create new problems. They are not for real use or for sale.*
  2 *At least 500.*

  Pronunciation: Kawakami /kɑwɑˈkɑmi/   Chindogu /tʃɪnˈdoʊgu/

b • Have students read the article again and complete the sentences in their own words. They could compare their answers with a partner before the follow up.

- Follow up by asking random students for their answers.

  AK 1 *...cat slippers and the back-scratcher T-shirt.*
  2 *...it solves an everyday problem, but creates another.*
  3 *...he was frustrated with society's materialism.*
  4 *...it cannot be for real use or for sale / humor cannot be the only reason for the invention.*
  5 *...encourage new ideas and thinking...*

c • Have students find the words in the article and choose the correct definition. Remind them to read the complete sentence before deciding.

   • Follow up by asking random students for their answer and the reason they chose it.

   AK   2 *b*   3 *b*   4 *a*   5 *b*   6 *a*

d • Either have a quick class discussion or put students in small groups and ask each group to report on the feeling of the majority.

13 Writing and Speaking

a • Look at the pictures and the description. Have students match the description to the picture. (*The shoe umbrellas.*)

   • You could get students to speculate on what the other picture is. (*It is a man's tie with pockets on the back that hold pens, business cards, scissors, credit cards, etc.*)

b • Have students look at the list of possible problem areas. Brainstorm for a minute or two to get some ideas about what problems there might be. For example, do they turn off the alarm and then go back to sleep? Do they have problems finding a seat on the bus?

   • You could also review some useful phrases for this activity before they start, for example, *We could… Why don't we…? What about…?* etc. or get students to brainstorm the kind of language they might need.

   • Put students in pairs to decide on the problem and invent a Chindogu.

c • Have students write a short description of their Chindogu, using the description in section 13a as a model. They could also draw a picture of their Chindogu.

d • Have students present their Chindogu to the class or to a group of students. They should begin by explaining the problem and then telling how the Chindogu will solve the problem. Encourage the other students to ask questions.

   • **Option:** The Chindogu ideas could be grouped together on posters, according to the problems they solve, and displayed around the room so that the students could read all of them.

6 Interesting characters

Main aims of this unit

Grammar: Present perfect simple vs. simple past; gerunds as subjects and after prepositions

Vocabulary: Prepositions with verbs and adjectives; adjective prefixes

Functions: Meeting and introducing people

Unit Overview

Reading:	Types of Friends
Speaking:	Describing types of friends
Vocabulary:	Prepositions with verbs and adjectives
Listening:	A discussion about friends
Focus on Grammar:	Present perfect simple vs. simple past
Language in Action:	Meeting and introducing people
KnowHow :	Pronunciation of the schwa /ə/
Listening:	Song
Listening:	An interview about personality tests
Focus on Grammar:	Gerunds as subjects and after prepositions
Vocabulary:	Adjective prefixes (*un-*, *dis-*, *im-*)
Speaking:	Analyzing handwriting
Reading:	Embrace Your Eccentricity
Writing:	Describing an interesting or unusual person

Warm-up

Ask students to think of a friend they have known for a long time or a friend they made recently. Ask them to tell the person beside them a little about this friend. This should be very quick.

1 ▶ Reading

a • Look at the list of types of friends and get students to speculate about what each type is like. Can they say anything about the relationship between the people in the pictures?

b • Have students read the article and fill in the blanks with the types of friends from 1a. Students could compare their answers with a partner before the follow-up.

• Follow up by asking random students for an answer and ask them to give the words or phrases which helped them decide.

> **AK** 2 *Train or Bus Friend* 3 *Ex-Friend* 4 *Wild Friend*
> 5 *Best Friend* 6 *Special-Interest Friend*

> **Language Note:** You could point out some of the following expressions in the article:
>
> *(someone) who can do no wrong:* This means that you always approve of what this friend does.
>
> *who you are, as opposed to who you were:* This implies that with a new friend you don't have to worry about what you were like in the past.
>
> *always there for you:* This means that the person is always willing to help you.

• Either have a class discussion or put students into pairs or small groups to talk about their friends. Circulate and listen.

• As a follow-up, ask the whole class what different categories of friends they came up with during their discussions. List these on the board.

2 Speaking

a • Put students in pairs to choose a type of friend from the list (or their own idea). Refer to the list you put on the board from 1c for more ideas.

> **Language Note:** The expression *old friend* refers to a person who has been a friend for a long time. It does not refer to the friend's age.

• Tell students to describe this kind of friend, using the paragraphs in the article to help. They should make notes, not write a whole paragraph.

b • Put students in small groups to describe the type of friend they chose. Encourage the listeners to make comments and ask follow-up questions.

• Follow up by asking each group for one example.

• **Option:** In a small class, you could have students make an oral presentation for the whole class.

3 Vocabulary: Prepositions with verbs and adjectives

a • Explain that certain expressions with verbs and adjectives require a particular preposition to complete the expression. There are no predictable rules about which preposition to use. These expressions are usually listed and explained in dictionary entries under the entry for the main word.

• Get students to complete as many expressions in the chart as they can. Then ask them to look at the article on page 43 to check their answers and find any expressions they don't know. They could do this in pairs.

> **AK** Verbs: *agree with*   *depend on*   *listen to*   *ask about*
> Adjectives: *interested in*   *surprised at*

b • Have students fill in the blanks with the correct prepositions. Follow up by asking random students for the complete sentence.

> **AK** 2 *on*   3 *to*   4 *with*
> 5 *about*   6 *at*

> **Optional Activity:** Get students to make their own true sentences with these expressions and record them in their notebooks. You could ask them to set aside a page to record any other verbs or adjectives with prepositions as they come across them.

4 ▶ Listening

a • Look at the picture and get students to describe Russell /ˈrəsəl/ and Audrey /ɔˈdri/.

• **AUDIO** Tell students they are going to listen to these people talking about their friends. They should listen and answer the question *What is the main difference between their ideas about friends?* Play the recording straight through.

• **AUDIO** Check the students' answers. If there is any disagreement, play the conversation again, pausing at the relevant points.

> **AK** *Russell's friends are mainly from work.*
> *Audrey's are mainly from outside work.*

b • Read through the statements. Ask *Which person might say each one?* Don't accept or reject any suggestions at this point.

• **AUDIO** Tell students to listen again to check their ideas and decide on any they were unsure of and make notes about the reasons. Pause the recording from time to time if necessary.

• **Option:** If students find it too challenging to write the names and the reasons at the same time, divide this task into two stages. Have them listen first just to write the names. Then play the recording again for them to make notes about the reasons.

• **AUDIO** Follow up by asking random students for their answers and the reasons for them. If there is any doubt or disagreement, play the recording again, pausing after Russell and checking which statements he might say. Then play the recording of Audrey and check her statements.

> **AK** *For the reasons, accept any reasonable response. These are the most likely answers.*
> 2 *Russell (His best friend lives in a different city.)*
> 3 *Both (Russell: Gary is one of his oldest friends. Audrey: She's known her best friend Lisa since she was six years old.)*
> 4 *Russell (He plays basketball, and there's an office soccer team.)*
> 5 *Audrey (She is a musician and plays in a band. The other band members are really good friends.)*
> 6 *Russell (He says it's more practical, since they spend so much time together anyway.)*

c • Either have a class discussion or put students in pairs or small groups to give their answer to the question and explain why.

- Follow up by having a show of hands to see whether more students have ideas similar to Russell's or to Audrey's.

5 ▶ Focus on Grammar

a • Look at the chart and get students to answer the questions.

> **AK** 1 *Simple past (completed action)*
> 2 *Present perfect simple*
> 3 *Use* ago *with the simple past. Use* for *with a period of time. Use* since *with a starting point in time.*

> **Optional Activity:** Write the following time phrases on the board in random order: *last year, a minute, three years, last month, yesterday, a long time, Tuesday, a while, two weeks, this morning.* Ask students to make two lists under the headings *for* and *since*.

> **Language Note:** *Since* is almost always used with the present perfect. The meaning of the word *since* is "from a particular time to (usually) the present." However, *for* is often used with other tenses as well. For example, *I lived there for 20 years. They're going to stay for three days.*

b • Do the first sentences with the class as an example to make sure they understand what they have to do.

- Have students write complete sentences with the prompts. They could compare with a partner before the follow-up.

- Follow up by asking random students for their answers and why they chose the verb tense. See the Language Note above about *for* and *since*. If a student uses the simple past in a sentence with *for,* you could explain that this is not incorrect. However, the purpose of this exercise is to practice using *for* with the present perfect.

> **AK** 2 *Ernesto got that job three years ago.*
> 3 *Melissa started an Italian class last week.*
> 4 *They have known Pete and Irene for ten years.*
> 5 *Our parents have lived in the same house since 1979.*
> 6 *Yoko and Alicia have worked together since June.*

c • Elicit one or two examples of questions and answers from the class. Have one student ask a question using one of the verbs on the list along with one of the nouns. Then have another student give a response.

- Have students continue asking and answering questions in pairs. Circulate and check.

- Follow up by asking random students for the most interesting fact they learned about their partner.

> **Optional Activity:** Ask students to record their partner's answers. This will give them a personalized record of the grammar points.

6 ▷ Language in Action: Meeting and introducing people

a • Look at the picture. Tell students they are going to listen to the three people talking, and that one of them is going to introduce the others.

• **AUDIO** Play the recording straight through. Students should listen and say what each person's name is and which person has seen Annie in the library.

> **AK** *The people are Daniel, Philip, and Annie.*
> *Philip has seen Annie before in the central library, where she works.*
> *(But they haven't met before.)*

> **In the Know:** To *hike* means to go for a long walk in the country, especially in a wilderness area. There are clubs called "hiking clubs" for people who enjoy this activity, so that they can go in groups.

b • Read through the expressions in the chart and check that students understand them.

• **AUDIO** Tell students to listen and check the expressions they hear. Play the recording straight through.

• **AUDIO** Follow up by asking random students which expressions they checked. If there is any doubt or disagreement, play the recording again, pausing after each expression.

AK

Introducing People	Recognizing Someone
I'd like you to meet…	I think we've met before.
✓ This is (name).	✓ Have we met before?
Do you know (name)?	✓ You look familiar.
Have you met (name)?	I think I recognize you.
✓ It's nice to meet you.	✓ That's why I recognize you.

c • *Help Desk:* Read through the Help Desk with the students. Ask them to suggest other pieces of information they could give when introducing someone, for example, their job, family, or how they met.

• Read through the example and then put students in groups to take turns introducing people. Tell them to try to give interesting pieces of information about the person they introduce, so that they avoid repetition of *We study English together.*

• Students should use as many expressions from the chart as they can. To encourage this, you could give each group a different expression on a slip of paper and tell them they have to include this in the conversation in some way.

> **Pronunciation:** Hugo /'hyugoʊ/   Lea /'liə/

• Follow up by asking if anyone learned something new about a classmate. Groups might also present conversations to the whole class.

7 ▸ *KnowHow*: Pronunciation of the schwa /ə/

> **Language Note:** The schwa is a very relaxed sound that occurs in English with unstressed vowels. This is why the sound can occur with any of the vowels. The schwa never occurs in stressed vowels.

a • Read the paragraph about the schwa sound with the students.

• Tell students to look at the underlined syllables in the words and phrases and say which vowels can be pronounced with the schwa sound.

• **AUDIO** If the students are not sure of the pronunciation of the schwa sound, you could play part of the recording now.

> ***AK*** *All the vowels (a, e, i, o, u) can be pronounced with the schwa sound.*

b • Get students to try to underline the schwa sound in the words given. If they are having difficulty with this, remind them that the schwa is always on the unstressed syllable. They could say the words quietly to themselves to "test" this.

• **AUDIO** Play the recording for them to listen and check.

> ***AK*** *advice   cousin   machine   tonight*
> *recognize   problem   similar   adventure*

- Have students repeat the sentences from 7a after the recording. Practice saying the words in 7b.

- **Option:** It is easier to produce the correct sound in a sentence. You could get students to make their own sentences with these words or give your own. For example, *She gave me good advice. Mary's my cousin. I can't work this machine. Let's go out tonight.*

8 ▸ Listening: Song

a • Have students read the song and try to fill in the blanks with the lines given. They could do this in pairs. (If they're having difficulty getting started, you could hint they look for words with similar sounds, i.e., rhyming words.)

- **AUDIO** When students have finished, or done as much as they can, play the recording straight through so that they can check their own answers.

> **AK**   2 *a*
> 3 *b*
> 4 *e*
> 5 *c*

b • **AUDIO** Have students read the questions. Play the recording straight through. Then have students answer the questions.

- Follow up by asking random students for answers. Ask them to say which lines of the song support their answers.

> **AK**   *Possible answers:*
> 1 *Friends are very important. (Lines 5 and 6)*
> 2 *No, she doesn't. She hopes for new friends in the future.*

> **Language Note:** *You got to* means *You have got to* or *you have to.* This kind of short form is very common in song lyrics. The students will also find *gotta* (got to), *gonna* (going to), and *wanna* (want to) written in lyrics. Tell them they should understand these but never write them! Even saying words this way could be a problem in very formal situations.

c • Brainstorm the songs students know on the topic of friends. These could be in English or in their own language. Ask them what each song says about friends and friendship.

9 ▶ Listening

a • Look at the pictures and have students speculate on what the personality tests shown involve. If necessary, give some help by asking questions such as *Do you think it's scientific? What does it base the test on?*

   • Ask students if they know of any other types of personality tests.

   > **Pronunciation:** graphology /græˈfɑlədʒi/
   > phrenology /frɛˈnɑlədʒi/
   > astrology /əˈstrɑlədʒi/

b • **AUDIO** Tell students to listen to the interview from a TV program and answer the question *Which kind of test from the picture is <u>not</u> discussed?* Play the recording straight through.

   • **AUDIO** Check answers with the class. If there's any disagreement, play the recording again.

   AK   *Astrology.*

c • Read through the questions with the students. Ask if they have ideas about what the answers might be before they listen.

   • If students can answer any of the questions, don't confirm or deny their answers.

   • **AUDIO** Play the recording again for students to listen either to check their responses or answer the questions. If necessary, pause the recording at appropriate points for students to make notes. (As usual, try to get students to focus first only on listening, not on writing responses. Reassure them that you'll allow time for writing later.)

   • **AUDIO** Follow up by asking random students for answers. Try to get several students to contribute information for questions that have more than one response. For example, there are several reasons for people to use personality tests. Make notes of the students' input on the board in order to put together a complete response. If there is any doubt or disagreement, play the recording again, pausing at appropriate points.

AK *Possible answers:*
1 *medical reasons* OR *employers wanting to know more about potential employees* OR *personal reasons*
2 *Graphology is the analysis of handwriting to learn about personality.*
3 *Personality is very complex.*
4 *Phrenology is the study of the bumps on the head to learn about personality.*

d • Either have a class discussion or put students in small groups to discuss the questions.

• Follow up by asking each group to give the majority opinion for questions 1 and 2. If anyone knows more about personality tests, ask them to share with the class.

10 Focus on Grammar

a • Look at the chart and the sentences below it. Get students to answer the question *In which sentence is the gerund used as subject?*

AK *Sentence 2.*

> **Language Note:** Remember that a gerund is the *-ing* form of the verb used as a noun. When the *-ing* form of a verb occurs in a continuous verb form, it is not a gerund. For example, *I **was driving** my car the other day.* (past continuous) BUT ***Driving** my car is enjoyable.* (gerund)

b • Have students form sentences by matching the two columns. This could be done individually and compared with a partner before the follow-up.

• Follow up by asking random students for answers. As they answer, you could ask in which sentences the gerund is used as a subject and in which it is used after a preposition.

AK 2 *c*   3 *a*   4 *b*   5 *d*

c • Give students time to make up sentences about themselves. Put students in pairs to compare their sentences. Circulate and check.

• Encourage students to ask follow-up questions. For example, if a student says *Eating chocolate isn't good for you,* his or her partner could ask *Why do you say that?*

• Follow up by asking random students for their partner's most interesting sentence.

11 ▸ Vocabulary: Adjective prefixes (*un-*, *dis-*, *im-*)

a • Tell students to look at the samples of handwriting and the analysis. Go over any unfamiliar words used to describe the handwriting, for example, *slant, T-bar, stroke, loop, braced*. Then have them underline the personality adjectives.

> **AK** *friendly   outgoing   popular   shy   generous   ambitious enthusiastic   honest   intelligent   stubborn*

• Follow up by asking random students for their answers. Check students' understanding of the vocabulary. It is all explained in the analysis.

> **Optional Activity:** If you feel that students need more practice with the vocabulary, you could give more examples of behavior and ask them to say which adjective fits the person you describe. For example, *When my brother has decided to do something, it's almost impossible to persuade him to do something different. (stubborn) My sister finds it difficult to meet new people. (shy)*

b • Get students to put the words in the correct category. Tell them to guess any they don't know. Suggest that they compare with prefixes in their own language.

• **AUDIO** Follow up by playing the recording so that students can check their lists.

AK

un-	dis-	im-
unfriendly	disorganized	impatient
unenthusiastic	disagreeable	impolite
unkind	dishonest	
unpopular		
unintelligent		

c • Get students to fill in the blanks with a negative adjective. They could compare with a partner before the follow-up.

• Follow up by asking random students for their answers.

> **AK** 2 *unenthusiastic*   3 *dishonest*
>   4 *disorganized*   5 *impatient*

> **Optional Activity:** Students could write personalized sentences in their notebooks, using all the adjectives to help them remember.

12 Speaking

a • Put students in pairs to prepare the analysis of the three handwriting samples. Make sure they refer back to the chart in 11a for ideas on how to analyze the samples.

• Circulate and listen, but don't interfere unless you are asked for help. The main focus here is on fluency and communication.

b • Put pairs together to make groups. They should take turns in presenting their analysis and compare and contrast them.

• Follow up by asking groups which sample(s) they agreed on. Ask groups for their analysis of one sample they agreed on. Then ask if they disagreed on any sample, and if so, why?

13 Reading

a • Elicit from students the meaning of the word *eccentric*. You might give an example of someone you know or have heard about who is eccentric. Then have students describe the people in the pictures and say what they think makes these people eccentric.

b • Tell students that the article is about some serious research into eccentricity.

• Have students read the article quickly to find some positive aspects of being eccentric.

• Follow up by asking random students for their answers. If there is any disagreement about what is a "positive aspect," have students give reasons and examples to support their answers.

> **AK** *Possible answers:*
> *Eccentric people live longer and are usually happier, healthier, and more intelligent than average people. (The article also mentions that eccentrics are creative, idealistic, and curious—characteristics most people would consider positive.)*

> **In the Know:** The article mentions *underwater basket-weaving* to give an exaggerated or improbable example of an eccentric activity. Basket-weaving is still practiced today; however, doing this activity underwater would be quite unusual.

Language Note: A common way to show possession with names ending in -s is to add an -'s, for example, *Dr. Weeks's conclusions*. However, another way to show possession is to add only an apostrophe, for example, *Dr. Weeks' study*. The original author of this article used only the apostrophe, and this style has been kept in this case. Elsewhere in this series, the apostrophe + s (-'s) has been used.

c • Tell students to read the article again, more slowly, and complete the statements in their own words.

• Elicit answers from volunteer students. Ask students to support their answers by referring to the article.

Note: Students may not be able to avoid using words and expressions from the article to complete the statements.

> **AK** *Possible answers:*
> 1 *...longer than other people.*
> 2 *...nonconforming, creative, obsessed by curiosity, idealistic, obsessed with one or more hobbies, intelligent, opinionated, and convinced that he or she is right.*
> 3 *...they like it OR it gives them pleasure.*
> 4 *...among the highest 15% of the general population.*
> 5 *...they experience much lower levels of stress because they don't feel the need to conform.*

d • Have students match the words from the article with the definitions. This could be done in pairs.

• Remind students to read the whole sentence before deciding on the definition.

> **AK** 1 *e*   2 *f*   3 *a*   4 *c*   5 *b*   6 *d*

e • Either have a class discussion or put the students into small groups. Stress that their examples don't need to be as eccentric as the people shown in the pictures. You might start things off by offering one or two examples of people you know.

• If students worked in groups, follow up by asking each group for their opinion of Dr. Weeks's conclusions and the most interesting eccentric they talked about.

14 Writing

a • Ask students to think of the most interesting or unusual person they know. Tell them they are going to describe this person to another student, so they should think of the reasons this person is special.

• Tell students they are going to write a paragraph about the person their partner describes. Have them think of questions they could ask to get detailed information from their partner.

• Put students in pairs to describe the person and answer their partner's questions. Make sure students take notes of the details they find out.

b • Have students write a paragraph about the person their partner described. Tell them to use the example to help.

• You could assign this for homework or do the writing in class.

c • Put students in the same pairs again and have them exchange the paragraphs. Ask the pairs to decide how accurate the descriptions are.

• **Option 1:** After students have discussed the content and given each other help to make the paragraphs more accurate, they could then look at the language and help each other correct any mistakes or rephrase sentences to make the meaning clearer. You could help with this as well.

• **Option 2:** To round off the unit you could display the paragraphs around the room and let students read all of them.

Units 4–6 Review

Grammar

1 *Possible answer:*
Look carefully at the person, and look for an interesting or unusual feature. Then connect that feature to the name.

2 2 *recognized*   3 *was shining*   4 *felt*
  5 *was standing*   6 *came*   7 *asked*

3 2 *My apartment is as big as Kate's (apartment).*
    OR Kate's apartment is as big as my apartment.
  3 *My sister is less absent-minded than I am.*
  4 *That guitar is more expensive than this guitar.*
  5 *My job is not (isn't) as difficult as your job.*

4 2 *Harry's wife, Sandra, wrote a novel that (OR which) has sold very well.*
  3 *Harry and Sandra have a son who (OR that) is 12 years old.*

5 2 *I have (I've) been here for 15 years.*
  3 *Did you go to Venezuela last year?*
  4 *I have not (haven't) gone to Venezuela since 1997.*

6 *Answers will vary.*

7 1 *were getting*   2 *it off*   3 *jacket that*
  4 *changing*   5 *them away*   6 *for*

Vocabulary

8 2 *First-class*   3 *full-time*   4 *brand-new*   5 *good-looking*

9 2 *to*   3 *to*   4 *about*   5 *about*
  6 *in*   7 *at*   8 *on*

Recycling Center

10 2 *do not (don't) understand*   3 *is looking*
  4 *tastes*   5 *am ('m) doing*

Fun Spot

out<u>*land*</u>*ish*   *ha*<u>*ndle*</u>   <u>*part*</u>*-time*   <u>*rea*</u>*listic*   <u>*leat*</u>*her*

7 Trade and treasure

Main aims of this unit

Grammar: Tag questions: Simple present and simple past; future forms: *will* vs. *be going to*

Vocabulary: Money; expressions with *make* and *do*

Functions: Transactions

Unit Overview

Listening:	A story about a lottery ticket
Vocabulary:	Money
Focus on Grammar:	Tag questions: Simple present and simple past
Speaking:	Sayings about money
Reading:	The Gift
Language in Action:	Transactions
Listening:	An interview about bartering
Vocabulary:	Expressions with *make* and *do*
In Conversation:	"I'll take a look at it if you want."
Focus on Grammar:	Future forms: *will* vs. *be going to*
KnowHow:	Dealing with mistakes
Writing and Speaking:	Finding people to barter with
Reading, Speaking, and Writing:	Solving treasure-hunting clues

Warm-up

Ask students how many different ways of getting money they can think of. Ask them which they think are easier and which are more difficult.

1 ▷ Listening

a • Look at the pictures. Have students identify the lottery ticket and the tip. Ask them how they think these pictures might be related to a movie. Have them speculate about the story. (If anyone in the class has actually seen the movie, you might ask them not to reveal everything they know about it right away!) Make some notes of their comments on the board to refer to later.

> **In the Know:** The movie *It Could Happen to You*, starring Nicolas Cage and Bridget Fonda, was directed by Andrew Bergman in 1994.

b • **AUDIO** Tell students they are going to listen to two people talking about the movie. Play the recording straight through. They should check their ideas about the story.

• Follow up by asking students how many of their ideas were correct. Refer back to the notes from 1a. Did they identify any of the elements in the story?

c • Make sure students understand that, in the conversation, the woman is talking about the movie and the man is talking about the true story.

• Look at the statements in the chart. Ask students *Which of these happened in the movie, in real life, or in both?* Let students say what they can remember, but don't confirm or deny any of their suggestions.

• **AUDIO** Play the recording again straight through. Ask them to listen again to check their ideas and decide on the ones they don't remember.

AK

	Movie	Real Life
2	✓	✓
3		✓
4	✓	
5		✓
6	✓	

- **AUDIO** Follow up by asking random students for their answers. If there is any doubt or disagreement, play the recording again, pausing at appropriate points for the students to check.

d • Ask students *What is the title of the movie? Can you explain it? Do you think it's a good title? Why / Why not?*

2 Vocabulary: Money

a • Tell students to read the paragraph and underline (or make a list of) the words and expressions related to money.

> AK save   spend   waste   buy   afford
>   lend   borrow   owe   pay back

- Check that students understand these verbs by asking them to give a synonym or an explanation.

> **Language Note:** Here are some simple definitions of the money words in the paragraph.
>
> *earn*: receive money for work
>
> *save*: keep money in a bank or some other safe place
>
> *spend*: use money to buy things
>
> *waste*: use money unnecessarily or to spend more than necessary
>
> *afford*: have enough money to buy something
>
> *lend (to)*: give something to someone temporarily expecting it to be returned
>
> *borrow (from)*: take something from someone, expecting to return it
>
> *owe*: be in debt
>
> *pay money back*: return money that you borrowed

- **_Help Desk:_** Read through the example sentences. Have students produce more sentences with *lend* and *borrow*. For example, *I lent my book to my friend. Could you lend me your dictionary, please? I borrowed my father's car when mine broke down.*

Optional Activity: Prepare (or have students prepare) one card for each student in the class with lists of three items they want to borrow and three that they have available to lend. (All imaginary, of course.) Items should vary widely in value. For example, one card might contain this text:

You want to borrow these items: a pencil, a sweater, a car.

You have these items to lend: a dictionary, a pen, a bicycle.

Have students circulate around the class trying to find people who can lend them the items they want to borrow and responding to people who want to borrow things from them. They can only borrow or lend the items on their card. If someone asks for something that is not on the card, they have to say something like, *Sorry, I don't have a….* At the end of the activity, students should report to the class some of things they borrowed or lent: *I borrowed a pen from Mike. I lent my bicycle to Sue.*

b • Have students fill in the blanks. Follow up by asking random students for their answers.

AK A: 2 *save*   3 *can't afford*   4 *waste*   5 *buy*
       B: 1 *borrow*   2 *lend*   3 *pay…back*

Language Note: With most two-word verbs, the object can be put between the two words or after them. *I paid my friend back.* OR *I paid back my friend.* But when the object is a pronoun, it **must** go between the two words. *I paid him back.* NOT ~~I paid back him~~.

Optional Activity: You could ask students to write their own sentences using the verbs and record them in their notebooks. This would give them a personalized record.

3 ▶ Focus on Grammar

a • Look at the chart. Point out the tag questions and explain that they are used to check information or ask for agreement.

> **Optional Activity:** You could have students look at the tag questions in the audioscript for Section 1 and find the answers to see how tag questions are used. (*...didn't he? Yes, he did.* / *...wasn't it? Really? I didn't know that.* / *...isn't it? Yes, it is.* / *...doesn't it? Yes, it does.*)

• Have students circle the answers in rules 1 and 2.

> **AK** 1 *be / do*   2 *negative / affirmative*

> **Language Note:** Occasionally, an affirmative tag can be used after an affirmative sentence, for example, *We are late again, are we?* This uncommon form is often used in an ironic or sarcastic sense.

• ***Help Desk:*** Read through with the students and have them supply short answers for the sentences in the grammar chart. (*Yes, it is. Yes, it was. Yes, it does. Yes, he did. No, it isn't. No, it wasn't. No, it doesn't. No, he didn't.*)

b • Have students match the beginnings and the tags. They could do this in pairs or individually and then check with a partner.

• Follow up by asking random students to give the complete sentence.

> **AK** 2 *c*   3 *d*   4 *f*   5 *h*   6 *a*   7 *b*   8 *e*

c • You could practice the intonation of tag questions before students start this activity. Use the tag questions on the recording as a reference. A tag question to check information has falling intonation. For example,

> *You live here, don't you?*

• Look at the example conversations. Ask a couple of students to suggest some other ideas for "opening" statements with tag questions. Then put students in pairs to make similar conversations on the suggested topics.

> **Optional Activity:** Ask students to think about what they know about you (place of origin, family, interests, etc.). Then ask them to check their ideas by making a statement followed by a tag question. They could also do the same thing in pairs.

4 Speaking

a • Look at the illustrations of fortune cookies with sayings related to money. Have students say what they think these sayings mean.

> **AK** Money makes the world go round: *Money is what makes the world function.*
> Never borrow from a friend: *Borrowing from a friend could end your friendship.*
> A fool and his money are soon parted: *Foolish people lose their money easily.*
> A penny saved is a penny earned: *If you save a little money, it is like earning more.*

• Give students time to think and write some of their own sayings about money. You could add these sayings: *Money is the root of all evil.* (Everything bad starts from money.) *Can't buy me love!* (Beatles song) *Time is money.* (Benjamin Franklin).

b • Work as a whole class (or if the class is big, you could divide into groups). Have students compare their sayings. They could write them on the board.

• Have a class discussion to try and agree on the three most popular sayings.

5 Reading

a • Tell students to look at the pictures, describe the woman, and speculate on what she did with her life savings. Accept any suggestions.

> **Pronunciation:** Oseola McCarty /oʊsiˈoʊlə məˈkɑrti/

• Have students read the first paragraph to check their guesses.

> **AK** *She gave her entire life savings to the University of Southern Mississippi.*

b • Tell students to read the whole article quickly to answer the question. Tell them not to worry about unknown vocabulary at this point.

• Follow up by asking students for their answer and evidence from the text.

> **AK** *It has received more than $300,000. (Paragraph 1: Her life savings were $150,000. Paragraph 7: Her gift has now been more than doubled—$150,000 x 2 = $300,000.)*

> **In the Know:** In the phrase *...she had only been out of the South once*, the expression *the South* means the southeastern states of the United States. The phrase *...who left school in sixth grade...* means she only went to school until she was about 11 or 12 years old. In the United States there are twelve years of school from elementary through high school. Most young people now have to stay in school until they are at least 16 years old. Most are 17 or 18 when they graduate from high school.

c • Look at the example. Ask students to find evidence for the answer in the text. Read through the other statements to check understanding.

   • Have students complete the exercise referring to the article as necessary. Ask them to read and check. This exercise could be done in pairs.

   • Follow up by asking random students for their answers and the reasons.

   AK 2 *No. In paragraph 2 she says "...with inflation, the price rose."*
        3 *No. Paragraph 4 says she never learned to drive and still walks everywhere.*
        4 *No. Paragraph 5 says she was afraid to fly but now she travels all over the country.*
        5 *No. Paragraph 5 says she has been the subject of many interviews and articles and she's visited the White House.*
        6 *Yes. In paragraph 6 she says "...I just want it to go to someone who will appreciate it and learn."*
        7 *No. In the last paragraph she says by giving the money away she is spending it on herself. This means that for her enabling a young person to go to college is giving her as much or more pleasure than anything she could buy for herself.*

d • When doing this exercise, remind students to first read the appropriate paragraphs to find the vocabulary items and then look at the definitions in order to choose the correct one. This exercise could be done individually and compared with a partner before the follow-up.

   • Follow up by asking random students for their answers and why they chose them.

   AK 1 *inflation*
        2 *accumulated*
        3 *frugally*
        4 *honored*
        5 *inspired*

e • Either have a class discussion or put students in small groups to discuss the questions. If you can think of an example of generosity that you know about, you could share this with the group to start the conversation.

• If students worked in groups, follow up by asking each group to summarize their answers.

6 Language in Action: Transactions

a • Look at the pictures and have students describe the situations. If necessary, ask *What have the two men done? Have they finished?* and *Where is the woman? What is she doing?*

• Read through the expressions in the chart. Don't explain what they mean at this time; tell students they will hear them in the conversations.

• Tell students they are going to listen to the conversations and number the expressions in the order they hear them.

• **AUDIO** Play the recording. You could either play both conversations or play one and check, then play the other and check.

AK	Paying in a Restaurant	Cashing a Check
	2 Let me get this.	3 Can I see some identification*, please?
	1 Can we have the check, please?	2 Can I cash this check, please?
	5 You paid last time.	1 Can I help you?
	4 It's too expensive.	5 Tens, please.
	3 It's my treat.	4 How would you like it? In (tens or twenties)?
	6 It's / This is on me.	

People commonly say "I.D." for identification.

b • **AUDIO** Look at the expressions and the example definition. Play the recording again. Tell students to listen and then explain what the other expressions mean.

• Follow up by asking the class for an explanation so that they work as a group to define the expressions.

> **AK** *Possible answers:*
> It's my treat *means "I want to pay for this as a present for you."*
> How would you like it? *means "What kind of bills do you want?"*
> Tens, please *means "I want (U.S.) $10 bills."*

c • Put students in pairs to practice the conversation in a restaurant. Then change pairs to practice the conversation for cashing a check.

Note: A quick way of changing pairs is to ask the person sitting at one end of the row to move to the other end and talk to the person there. The other students then work with the person on the other side of them from their first partner.

> **Optional Activity:** You could set up a large role-play for the bank conversation. Make a third or less of the class tellers and the others customers so that you have small lines at the tellers' windows. Tell students to chat in English (informal social expressions, complaining about having to wait, etc.) while they wait in line to cash their checks. Then as students get to the "window," they role-play the conversation with the teller.

7 ▶ Listening

a • Read the definition of *barter* and make sure students understand this. Ask if anything similar to bartering exists in their society. Have students exchange ideas about bartering.

b • Tell students they are going to listen to a conversation with a person who barters.

• **AUDIO** Play the recording straight through. Students should listen and answer the question *How does Luke feel about bartering?*

• Follow up by asking students for their answer and the reasons.

> **AK** *He likes it. He says it's a good option for people who don't have a lot of money, and he enjoys it.*

c • Read through the questions with the students. If they can answer any from memory, don't accept or reject their ideas but ask them to check when you play the recording.

• **AUDIO** Play the recording again. Tell students to listen but not to make notes at this time.

- After students have listened to the recording, go through the questions again. Ask volunteers to contribute anything they heard that might relate to any of the questions. Write notes on the board. Encourage students to discuss possible answers.

- **AUDIO** Play the recording again pausing at appropriate moments to allow the group to check the information and answer the questions.

Note: Approaching the listening task in this way helps build student confidence, as students collaborate on the task.

> ***AK*** 1 *He started to barter with a friend who used to barter for everything.*
> 2 *He knows a lot of people because of his job. He's a house painter.*
> 3 *Because they didn't agree on everything in advance. (Also because the other person wanted too much in return for helping Luke with his computer. He wanted him to "paint his whole house.")*
> 4 *He has bartered for hair cuts, food and meals, help with his computer, furniture, car repairs, and a truck.*
> 5 *Because he was bartering too much, and he wasn't making enough money.*

d • Have a class discussion to exchange opinions.

8 Vocabulary: Expressions with *make* and *do*

a • Read through the instructions with the students and make sure they understand the hint.

> **Language Note:** The word *make* can mean:
> to produce something, for example, *make a dress, make a cup of coffee*
>
> to perform an action, for example, *make a discovery, make an effort, make a promise*
>
> to cause something to happen, for example, *They made me wait a long time. Don't make me laugh.*

- You could put students in pairs to try to put the expressions with the correct verbs.

b • **AUDIO** When students have finished, play the recording for them to check their answers. Give them time to make any corrections.

> **AK** make: *a profit*   *a mistake*   *a living*   *friends*
> *a decision*   *a list*   *noise*   *a meal*
> do: *a job*   *someone a favor* *housework or chores*
> *laundry*   *the shopping*   *business*

c • Tell students to do this exercise first without referring back to exercise b. Then have students check with the lists they made in exercise b.

• Tell students to read the information about bartering and choose *make* or *do*.

> **AK** 1 *make*   2 *make*   3 *make*   4 *make*
> 5 *Make*   6 *do*   7 *do*   8 *make*

9 ▶ In Conversation

• Look at the picture. Have students describe the people and say what they think the woman is trying to do.

• **AUDIO** Ask students to close their books and listen to answer the question *What do they agree to do and when?* Play the recording straight through.

• Ask students what they think the answers are, but don't accept or reject any suggestions.

• **AUDIO** Tell students to open their books and read the conversation. Play the recording again while they are reading.

> **AK** *They agree that Chuck will fix the air conditioner on Sunday and then Sheila will buy him dinner.*

10 ▶ Focus on Grammar

a • Ask students to find and underline all the examples of *will* and *be going to* in the conversation in section 9.

• Tell students to look at the chart and choose the correct answers to complete the rules.

• Read through the completed rules with the students. Point out the use of *will* when something is uncertain or undecided.

> **AK** 1 *be going to*   2 *will*

b • Have students complete the two conversations with *will* or *be going to*.

• Follow up by asking random students for their answers and why they chose them.

AK 1 *I'll help... (decision made at the time of speaking)*
        I'm going to start... (plan)
        I'll come... (decision made at the time of speaking)
    2 *...are you going to do (asking about plans)*
        I'll go... I'll work... (uncertain)
        I'm going to meet... (plan)

c • Put students in pairs to make conversations about their plans for the next week. Circulate and listen. Follow up by asking some pairs to repeat their conversations for the class.

11 *KnowHow*: Dealing with mistakes

a • Have a class discussion about making mistakes. Make sure students understand that making mistakes is a part of learning, not something to be ashamed of. Explain that if they only say or write what they are sure is correct, they will not make as much progress as they would if they took risks and experimented.

• Ask students about mistakes they commonly make. Note those mistakes mentioned by more than one person.

b • Look at the suggested strategies for dealing with mistakes. Ask students if they have tried any of them before and if they can add other ideas. This could be done in small groups, especially if the class is big.

• You could follow up by making a list on the board of the students' ideas for other strategies.

• If students are having difficulty thinking of strategies, suggest some of the following: Look in grammar books and dictionaries when you are checking written work. Don't be afraid to ask other people when you have doubts. Help other students, but don't overcorrect as this can be frustrating, especially when someone is speaking. Don't be afraid to experiment and take risks when you are speaking. You will soon know if people have understood what you want to say. Don't be afraid to say *No* when someone says *Do you understand?*

> **Optional Activity:** Ask students to copy the list into their notebooks and try out more later in the course or make a poster to stay on the wall. Other strategies could be added as they come up.

c • Ask students to use at least one of the suggested strategies as they do the activity in section 12.

• Brainstorm some useful phrases which students can use when correcting each other or asking for help and write them on the board. For example, *I got that wrong, didn't I? Did you get/understand what I meant? Do you mean…or…? I'm not sure of this. Can you help me?*

12 Writing and Speaking

a • Look at the notice. Ask students *What is the person offering? What does he or she need in return?*

• Tell students to think of a skill they can offer and one that they need. They can use real skills or the ideas on the list.

• Using the notice as a model, have students write their own notices.

b • Have students put up their notices.

• Read through the example conversation. Tell students to mingle to find people to barter with.

• Set a time limit of about six minutes, but be prepared to let it go longer if the students are communicating well.

c • Follow up by asking students to say who they are going to barter with and what they're going to exchange.

• Ask students which strategies from section 11 they used in the conversations and how they worked.

13 Reading, Speaking, and Writing

Note: A tourist-type map (if possible, one with illustrations) of your city would be very useful for the last part of this section.

a • Tell students to look at the pictures and speculate about what a treasure hunt is. Accept any suggestions at this point.

b • Tell students to read the flyer and fill in each blank with a title.

• Check that they understand that *What, When, Where,* and *How much* are abbreviated forms of the questions *What is it? When and where is it?* and *How much is it?* Also check that they understand that *What to bring* means what you should bring.

- Follow up by asking random students for their answers.

    AK 1 *What*   3 *When & where*   4 *How much*   5 *What to bring*

- Check that students understand what a treasure hunt is. If this is a completely new idea, have a short discussion to clarify any doubts.

> **In the Know:** In this type of treasure hunt, the teams receive one clue which brings them to the next location where another clue is waiting for them. They continue in this way until they reach the end and find the "treasure."

c • Use this exercise to check key vocabulary. Tell students to find each word in the text, read the phrase or sentence that includes it, and work out what it means. This could be done in pairs.

- Follow up by asking random students for their ideas.

    AK clues: *pieces of information which help to find the answer to a question*
    solve: *find the answer to a difficult question or problem*
    sharp *(5 p.m. sharp!): at exactly 5 o'clock*
    proceeds: *money gained from the sale of something (in this case, the sale of tickets)*

d • Look at the picture of the park. Have students identify as many things as possible.

- Tell students to read the sample clues, try to solve the puzzles, and find the places on the picture of the park. This could be done in pairs. Set a time limit of about three or four minutes.

> **In the Know:** The position of the hands on a traditional clock face can be used to communicate the location of a person or item. *Look to 12 o'clock* means "look straight ahead." *Look to 6 o'clock* means "look behind oneself." *Look to 9 o'clock* means "look to the left," and *Look to 3 o'clock* means "look to the right."

- After the time is up, ask students how they are doing. If most of them have ideas, continue with the follow-up. If not, offer help if necessary and give them a bit more time.

- Follow up by asking students for their answers and how they solved the clues.

AK A *The numbers represent the letters of the alphabet (A = 1, B = 2, C = 3, etc.), so the clue reads* Look in the flowers.

B *Under the bench on the left of the clock.* (Near a place of higher learning *refers to the university.* The time is always changing *refers to the clock.* Look to 9 o'clock *means look left.* …have a seat *refers to the bench.*)

e • Divide the class into teams. The teams should be small enough to ensure that all the students participate in the group.

• If you have a map of your area, ask them to use places shown on the map. If not, they can make clues for any public places in the area. Circulate and help as necessary.

• You could ask the teams to exchange only the first clue. When the opposing team has solved the first clue, they receive the others one-by-one, until they "find" the treasure.

> **Optional Activity:** If you have a map, you could make a wall display with the map in the center and the clues around it. The students could then try all the clues and perhaps other groups would be interested in trying to solve them.

8 *A taste of it*

Main aims of this unit

Grammar: Passive: Simple present and simple past; use of *the* and quantifiers

Vocabulary: Food preparation and cooking; common uncountable nouns

Functions: Explaining and giving reasons

Unit Overview

Speaking and Listening:	A food history quiz
Focus on Grammar:	Passive: Simple present and simple past
Listening:	Making potato chips
Vocabulary:	Food preparation and cooking
KnowHow:	Consonant clusters
Speaking:	Presenting a cooking show script
Language in Action:	Explaining and giving reasons
Listening:	A folk tale about salt
Vocabulary:	Common uncountable nouns
Focus on Grammar:	Use of *the* and quantifiers
Reading:	Ostrich Mania
Speaking and Writing:	A publicity brochure about local products

Warm-up

Ask students what they had for lunch (or dinner) yesterday. How many different dishes did the class have? Ask who prepared the meal.

Brainstorm all the vocabulary they can think of related to food and beverages. If necessary, lead them into tableware (knife, fork, etc.) and different kinds of drinks (tea, coffee, carbonated drinks, etc.).

1   Speaking and Listening

a • Tell students they are going to take a quiz about the history of food.

• Put students in pairs. Tell them to use <u>one</u> book for the quiz. (This helps to make sure they don't work individually.) They should discuss the answers with their partner.

• Tell them they must answer all the questions. If they don't know, they should agree on a guess.

> **Language Note:** *Carbonated beverages* contain carbon dioxide which produces bubbles. For example, soft drinks and sparkling water are carbonated beverages.

b • **AUDIO** Play the recording so that the students can check their own answers.

• Follow up by asking if there was any new and interesting information in the quiz.

> **AK**   1 *Italy*   2 *to Japan from China*   3 *India*   4 *Italy*
>   5 *Mexico*   6 *Spain*   7 *Switzerland*   8 *France*
>   9 *Brazil*   10 *France*

2   Focus on Grammar

a • Have students look at the examples and choose the correct answer.

> **AK**   *the process or action*

b • Ask students to look at the chart and say how the passive is formed.

> **AK**   *The passive is formed with a present or past form of the verb be + the past participle of the main verb.*

- Have students underline all the passive forms in the quiz on page 61. You could compare this with the students' own language, if it is appropriate. Is there a similar form? Is it used in the same way?

c • Look at the example with the students. Ask *Why is is used?* (*Rice* is uncountable and therefore singular.) Have students write passive sentences using the prompts.

- Follow up by asking random students for their answers.

> **AK** 2 *Potatoes were taken to Ireland from South America in 1588.*
> 3 *Corn is grown in many places in the United States today.*
> 4 *The sandwich was invented by the Earl of Sandwich in 1762.*
> 5 *The first apple trees were planted in North America in 1629.*
> 6 *Today, coffee is grown in 50 different countries.*

d • Read the example with the students.

- This activity could be done in pairs, in small groups, or with the whole class.

- If you are going to put students into groups or pairs, first elicit one or two examples from volunteer students to make sure they understand the activity. Follow up by asking random students to share their ideas with the whole class.

3 ▸ Listening

a • Look at the list of steps in the process of making potato chips and get students to say what they think happens in each step. Deal with any unknown vocabulary items at this point.

- Have students discuss the order in which they think the steps happen. Accept any suggestions.

b • **AUDIO** Tell students they are going to listen to a tour guide explaining the process of making potato chips to some visitors to the factory. They should listen and check their predictions in section 3a. Play the recording straight through.

- **AUDIO** Have students check their predictions from 3a. Were they correct? If there is any disagreement about the order, play the recording again.

> AK   1 *delivery and quality control*
> 2 *cleaning and peeling*
> 3 *cooking and seasoning*
> 4 *weighing, packaging, and shipping*

c • Read through the chart and ask students to complete any answers that they can remember. Tell students to write the numbers in figures, not words.

• **AUDIO** Play the recording again. Have students listen, check any answers they have written in, and complete the others.

• **AUDIO** Follow up by asking random students for their answers. If there is any doubt or disagreement, play the recording again, pausing at key points.

• As the answers involve some high numbers, you could ask students to write the numbers in figures on the board to check they have understood.

> AK   1 *About 130,000,000 lbs. (pounds) of potatoes*
> 2 *35,000,000 lbs. of chips*
> 3 *8 different states (and Canada)*
> 4 *1% rejected*
> 5 *10 flavors*

> **In the Know:** 1 kilo is about 2.2 lbs. Therefore, 130,000,000 lbs. would be about 59,000,000 kg., and 35,000,000 lbs. would be about 16,000,000 kg.

d • Have a class discussion about popular snack foods and how students think they are made.

4 Vocabulary: Food preparation and cooking

a • Look at the illustrations of the vocabulary. Point out the difference between *slice* and *chop*; *bake* and *roast*.

> **Language Note:** *Bake* and *roast* are both ways of cooking in an oven. *Roast* is used mostly for meat. *Bake* is used for things like bread, cookies, and cakes and generally for things being baked in a container of some sort.

• You could ask students for other examples of foods that they *slice, chop, peel, fry, boil, bake, roast, grill,* or *barbecue.*

• Have students divide the items into two lists: *Food preparation* and *Ways of cooking.*

- Follow up by asking random students for one item of vocabulary and which column it goes in. If there are any differences of opinion, ask students to explain their reasons.

> **AK** Food preparation: *chop, peel, mix*
> Ways of cooking: *boil, roast, bake, grill, barbecue*

- **Help Desk:** Read through the Help Desk with the students. Ask students if they can think of other types of food with adjectives that describe the way they are cooked. For example, *fried, boiled,* or *baked eggs; grilled* or *fried sausages.*

  - Ask students which ways of cooking they prefer for vegetables, meat, and fish.

b • Look at the recipes for Apple Pie and Egg Salad.

  - Tell students to fill in the blanks in each recipe with the words above it.

c • **AUDIO** Follow up by playing the recording for the students to check their answers.

> **AK** Apple Pie: 2 *slice*   3 *Add*   4 *mix*   5 *Bake*
> Egg Salad: 6 *Boil*   7 *Peel*   8 *chop*   9 *Add*   10 *Mix*

> **Language Note:** A *pie shell* is a pastry case used to contain the filling in a pie. *Cinnamon* is a spice often used when baking with apples or preparing other sweet foods.

5 ▸ *KnowHow*: Consonant clusters

a • **AUDIO** Play the recording, pausing for students to repeat after each word.

  - Do more repetition practice on any words that cause difficulty. If necessary, practice the clusters separately and then put them together in the words.

b • **AUDIO** Get students to say these words and then play the recording to check their pronunciation.

  - If necessary, do more repetition practice with these words.

c • Have students make a list of other words including the clusters given.

  - If students are having any difficulty, suggest they look in the vocabulary reference at the back of the book or give some examples from the previous levels: *stand, sleep, crackers, friend, great, bread, spell.*

- Put students in pairs to compare lists. Follow up by making a master list of all the words the class thought of.

> **Optional Activity:** Tongue twisters. Write these sentences (or make up your own) on the board and get students to try and say them.
> *Frank likes fried frankfurters.*
> *Steve steams sliced sausages.*
> *Chris creates crisp chips.*
> Students could also make up their own from the list of words they produced.

6 Speaking

a • Look at the picture and have students describe the situation. Ask students if TV cooking shows are popular and if they watch this type of program.

- Explain that they are going to write a script for a TV chef to prepare and demonstrate a recipe.

- Put students in pairs and give them two minutes to think of a dish.

- Read through the questions and tell students to use these to help as they write the script. Set a time limit of perhaps 20–30 minutes (or less) for writing the script.

- Circulate and help as necessary. If some pairs seem to be taking longer than the others, give them some suggestions to help them work more quickly.

- **Option:** If students are not particularly interested in cooking, they could produce a "recipe" for something other than food, not necessarily serious, for example, recipes for "magical" face creams or hair restorers.

b • Give students a few minutes to practice their presentations. Put students in groups to present their recipes to each other.

- Follow up by asking each group to say which recipe was the easiest, most difficult, and most unusual.

- **Option:** If time and classroom facilities allow, bring (or have students bring) in a few basic cooking utensils and set up a simulated "kitchen" on a table.

7 ▶ Language in Action: Explaining and giving reasons

a • Look at the picture and have students describe what is happening.

• Tell students they are going to listen to a conversation in which the people are talking about tea.

• **AUDIO** Play the recording straight through. Have students listen and answer the questions *What is the fact about tea?* and *What is the legend about tea?*

• **AUDIO** Check students' responses. If students have difficulty telling the story, ask several students to contribute any details they can remember. Note these on the board to help students retell the story. Play the recording again if necessary.

> **AK** Fact: *More tea is consumed around the world than any other beverage.* Legend: *About five thousand years ago, a Chinese emperor was boiling water under a tree when some leaves fell into the pot. He tasted the water and liked how it tasted. Because of that we drink tea today. (Students' wording will vary.)*

b • **AUDIO** Read through the expressions in the chart. Play the recording again. Tell students to listen again and check the expressions they hear.

• Follow up by asking random students for one of the expressions they heard. Ask if anyone can complete the sentence.

• Tell students they could look at the Audioscripts at the back of the book if they want to see the complete sentences.

AK

Asking and Explaining	Responding
✓ Did you know that…?	I'd never thought of that.
✓ Do you know that / how / why / where…?	✓ I didn't know that.
That's the reason that…	✓ I have no idea.
That's why / how…	✓ That explains a lot.
✓ Because of that…	
It's because of…that…	

c • Before students do this exercise, you could practice the pronunciation and intonation of the expressions in 7b.

- Have students look at the facts about tea. Then put them in pairs to use the expressions above to talk about tea. For example, A: *Did you know that there are more than 3,000 varieties of tea?* B: *No, I didn't know that.* / A: *Do you know how the tea bag was invented?* B: *Yes, It was created...*

- Follow up by asking some pairs to repeat their conversation for the class.

> **Optional Activity:** Tell students they are going to have conversations about the origin of something. Write some ideas on the board. For example, *the origins of coffee, the origins of chocolate, etc.* Have students look at the ideas and then brainstorm with the whole class to get a few more ideas.
>
> Put students in pairs to create their conversations. Emphasize that these should be short conversations, like the one in 7a, not long discussions. If it seems that students will not have enough information at hand to do this spontaneously, assign the preparation for homework and have students create the conversations in the next class. You could give students the following information about the origins of coffee as an example.
>
> *The origins of coffee:* It's generally agreed that coffee originated in Ethiopia. A legend says that a goatherd named Kaldi noticed that his goats started jumping around and were full of energy after eating the beans from a certain bush. He took some of the beans to a nearby monastery. The abbot became angry and threw the beans into the fire to destroy them. But the aroma from the roasting beans was so pleasant and filled him with so much energy that the monks eventually developed the idea of making a liquid drink from the roasted beans.

8 ▶ Listening

> **Optional Activity:** Write these expressions on the board and ask the students what they think they mean and if they have any similar expressions in their language.
>
> *salt of the earth*: An example of the type of person who is kind, honest, and not pretentious in any way.
>
> *to take with a grain of salt*: To be inclined to think that something is not completely true.
>
> *to be worth one's salt*: To be very valuable, usually in a professional way, very efficient and capable.
>
> Ask students if they know any other expressions related to salt, in English or in their own language

a • Tell students they are going to listen to a traditional folk tale and that all the things on the list fit into it. Check that students understand the vocabulary.

• Put students in pairs or groups to discuss how they think the things on the list might fit into the story.

• Follow up by asking groups for their ideas, but don't accept or reject any suggestions at this time. You could make notes on the board for students to refer to later, after they have listened to the recording.

b • **AUDIO** Tell students to listen to the story. Play the recording straight through. They should answer the question *What does the king learn in the story?* They can also check if their ideas from section 8a were correct. (Refer to the notes on the board.)

• Follow up by asking random students for their answers and by asking each group how close their ideas in 8a were to the story.

> **AK**   *The king learns how necessary salt is.*

c • Read through the aspects of the story and look at example 1. Tell students that while they listen again they should only make notes (write key words), not whole sentences, for 2–6.

• **AUDIO** Play the recording again straight through. Give students time to convert their notes into complete sentences.

• Follow up by asking random students for their sentences on the aspects of the story. You could ask other students for more details, if necessary. Go through all the aspects.

• **AUDIO** If there is any doubt or disagreement, play the recording again, pausing after each section for students to check.

> **AK**   *Possible answers: These answers are in the form of complete sentences with the key words underlined.*
> 2 *Two daughters brought presents that were necessary to human life, but were very expensive. The youngest daughter brought him a small pile of salt.*
> 3 *The king was very angry with his youngest daughter and sent her away.*
> 4 *She met a prince, fell in love, and agreed to marry him.*
> 5 *There was a big feast. The king was invited. The youngest daughter told the cooks to prepare all the food without salt.*
> 6 *The king realized how important salt was and was sad because he had sent his daughter away. She made herself known to him, and they all lived happily ever after.*

101

d • Put students in pairs to practice retelling the story in their own words and then discuss what they think the moral of the story is.

• Follow up by asking each pair for their idea of the moral. Avoid judging students' answers as right or wrong. There are many possible answers. Focus more on the reasons for the answers.

> **AK** *Possible answers:*
> *Not everything important is expensive. Simple things can be valuable. Sometimes we don't take enough notice of simple things. We sometimes only notice the value of simple things when they are not there.*

9 ▸ Vocabulary: Common uncountable nouns

a • Look at the chart headings and the examples in the categories. Read through the list of words with the students.

• Students could work in pairs to put the words in the correct categories. Follow up by asking random students for their answers.

> **AK** General classes of objects: *furniture, clothing*
> Liquids and solids: *water, milk, coffee, salt, bread*
> Abstract nouns: *information, love, beauty, honesty*
> Fields of study and languages: *mathematics, Japanese, history*

> **Language Note:** The nouns *economics*, *news*, and *linguistics* are uncountable and are singular even though they end in -*s*. For example, *Economics is the first class of the day. The news is usually interesting. Linguistics is the study of language.* BUT *Economics and linguistics are my only classes on Tuesday.*
>
> The word *fruit* can also be used as a countable noun. The uncountable form is used to refer to fruit in general. For example, *Should I buy some fruit?* The countable form is used when "a fruit" means "a type of fruit." For example, *Pineapples and papayas are tropical fruits.*

b • Put students in pairs to think of other nouns to add to the categories.

• Students could compare their lists of other nouns in small groups or as a class to make longer lists.

> **AK** *Possible answers:*
> *baggage, food*
> *butter, cheese, corn, glass, sugar, wheat*
> *luck, patience, health, homework*
> *biology, English, French, Portuguese*

- **Help Desk:** Remind students not to use *a / an* with uncountable nouns. You could ask students what to use instead. (*Some* OR *any.*)

- If students are in doubt about the use of *some / any*, practice a little before doing the next section.

> **Optional Activity:** Review of *some / any / a / an.* Write some sentences on the board and have students complete them with *some /any, a /an*, or *N* (nothing). For example, *My sister studies (-) history. Last week, she went to the library to find (-) information about (-) transportation for (-) project. She looked at (-) books, but she couldn't find (-) information about the first trains. At last, she found (-) information in (-) book about (-) American history.*
> Follow up by having students explain why their answers are correct.

10 ▸ Focus on Grammar

a • Tell students to look at the chart and choose the correct answers to complete the rules.

> **AK** 1 *Don't use*   2 *Use*   3 *countable*

- Read through the sentences in the chart and have students link each one to rule 1, 2, or 3.

b • Read the example with the students. Ask *Why is there no article here?* (*Because it is a generalization.*) Make sure students understand that *N* means that nothing goes in the blank.

- Have students fill in the blanks with *the* or *N*.

- Follow up by asking random students for an answer and the reason for it.

> **AK** 2 *the*   3 *the*   4 *N*   5 *the*   6 *N / N*   7 *N*

- **Help Desk:** Read through the note and the example sentences. Have students create their own sentences, using *few / a few* or *little / a little*.

c • Tell students to fill in the blanks with *a little, a few,* or *a lot of*.

- Follow up by asking random students for their answers and the reasons for them.

> **AK** 2 *a lot of*   3 *a little*   4 *a few*
>   5 *a lot of*   6 *a few*

d • Read through the examples.

> **In the Know:** *Junk mail* is usually advertising material that is sent to people even if they have not asked for it. The equivalent in e-mail is called *spam*.

• Tell students to make true sentences using the suggestions or their own ideas. You could put students in pairs to compare their sentences.

• Follow up by asking for some examples from the students.

> **Optional Activity:** The alphabet shopping game. Put students into small groups. The first person begins the game saying *I went to the store and bought (a few apples).* The person must use a word that starts with the letter *a.* The next person repeats what the first person said and adds an item with the next letter of the alphabet. Each item should also be preceded by *a few* or *a little,* depending on whether it is a countable or uncountable noun. (*I went to the store and bought a few apples and a little butter.*) The groups should work together to get as far as they can in the alphabet in a time limit of about four minutes. (This means that if someone has trouble remembering the list, the others can help him or her.)

11 ▶ Reading

a • Put students in pairs or groups to make a list of things they know about ostriches, using the questions to help.

> **Pronunciation:** ostrich /ˈɑstrɪtʃ/

• Follow up by asking each group for their lists. Were there any questions they couldn't answer or were not sure about?

• You could ask if they have any other things they'd like to know and write these questions on the board.

b • Have students read the article quickly to explain why the title is "Ostrich Mania." Accept any reasonable response that resembles the answer below in content.

> **AK** *The title is "Ostrich Mania" because in the late 1800s and early 1900s, ostrich farming was extremely popular in South Africa.*

• Tell students to read the article again and check their answers to the questions in section 11a. Do they agree with the information in the article? They could also see if there are any answers to their own questions from section 11a.

c • Students could do this exercise in pairs or individually and then compare with a partner.

   • Tell students to complete the sentences with information from the text.

   • Follow up by asking random students for their answers.

   > **AK** *The wording of the answers will vary. Possible answers:*
   > 1 ...*they don't fly and they don't sing. OR They swallow rocks and even diamonds. They kick and bite, which is unusual for birds.*
   > 2 ...*travelers confused ostriches with camels.*
   > 3 ...*women started to wear hats and other clothing decorated with ostrich feathers.*
   > 4 ...*the farmers wanted to show off their wealth.*
   > 5 ...*when World War 1 started, the fashions changed.*

d • Remind students to read the complete sentence that includes the word before choosing the correct definition.

   > **Pronunciation:** swallow /ˈswɑlouʊ/   adorn /əˈdɔrn/

   • Follow up by asking random students to read the complete definition they chose and say why they chose it.

   > **AK** 2 *f*   3 *b*   4 *c*   5 *d*   6 *g*   7 *a*

e • Explain that *mania, craze,* and *fad* all have a similar meaning. They refer to things that become very popular very quickly, to the point that people are almost "crazy" about them. Typically though, this popularity does not last very long.

   • If students have difficulty thinking of any fads, suggest some categories such as dances, items of clothing, hobbies, or games.

   • Have a quick class discussion about other fads and crazes the students have heard about.

12 Speaking and Writing

Note: It would be helpful if you can find some examples of information brochures or web sites about your country. These are often available from tourist agencies. The brochures don't need to be in English.

a • Look at the pictures and have students identify the different industries and products. Ask students about the industries and products of their country.

   • Have them work in groups to make lists of the products in each category.

b • Tell students they are going to produce an informational brochure about one of their country's products.

• Put students in groups. Tell them to choose a product and write a couple of paragraphs about it as if they were preparing text for a brochure. (The group should choose one product and work together to write about it.)

• **Option:** Students may feel they need to do some research for this. In this case you could continue the activity in the next class, after they have had time to investigate their product.

c • Have each group present their product to the class or to another group. This could be done orally or the paragraphs could be posted around the room for all students to read.

• Ask students to choose the paragraphs they feel best represent their country's products.

Optional Activity: When the groups have produced their paragraphs, ask them to add some illustrations. These could be postcards, pictures from brochures, or drawings. They should write captions for the illustrations. Stick the paragraphs and illustrations on pieces of paper and then staple them together to make brochures. OR Make zigzag-folded brochures that could be opened up and displayed on the wall of the classroom.

9 By land and by sea

Main aims of this unit

Grammar: Present perfect continuous; *used to*
Vocabulary: Travel expressions; prepositions and nouns
Functions: Making travel arrangements

Unit Overview

Listening:	Song
Speaking:	Discussing views on traveling
Listening:	Personal travel stories
Vocabulary:	Travel expressions
In Conversation:	"We've been walking around in circles."
Focus on Grammar:	Present perfect continuous
Language in Action:	Making travel arrangements
Writing:	A personal travel story
Reading:	A book review and extract from *8 Men and a Duck*
Vocabulary:	Prepositions and nouns
Listening:	A modern explorer
Focus on Grammar:	*Used to*
KnowHow:	Improving fluency
Speaking:	Creating an advertisement for a trip

Warm-up

Ask students *When you travel, how do you like to go? Do you travel by car? By bus? By plane?*

1 Listening: Song

a • **AUDIO** Ask students to cover the song or close their books and listen. Play the recording straight through. Ask the question *How does the singer feel about traveling?*

> **In the Know:** This song was written by Willie Nelson, a popular country western singer in the United States, who was the subject of a reading exercise in Unit 5.

• Follow up by asking random students for their answers. Ask students to support their answers with lines from the song.

   AK *He likes to travel.*

> **Language Note:** In informal speech it is common for the *-ing* at the end of a word to have a shorter sound. The word *going*, for example, becomes /'goɪn/, instead of /'goɪŋ/. The written form *goin'* (or *doin'*, *havin'*...) is used only when the writer is trying to represent real speech as in a song or in written dialog in a book.

b • **AUDIO** Have students look at the lyrics of the song. Point out that the lines in the middle section are in the wrong order. Tell them to listen again and number the lines in the correct order. Play the recording again.

• **AUDIO** Follow up by asking random students for the correct order. If there is any doubt or disagreement, play the recording again, pausing at the end of each of the eight lines for students to check.

AK   Order of lines: *8, 4, 5, 7, 1, 3, 2, 6*

> **In the Know:** *Gypsies* (or *gipsies*) /ˈdʒɪpsiz/ are people of Indian and eastern European origin who traditionally live traveling from place to place, often living and traveling in caravans. The word is also used to describe anyone who travels a lot.

2 ▶ Speaking

a • Read through the quotes about travel with the students and deal with any vocabulary problems.

• Put students in small groups to discuss what the quotes mean and if they agree or disagree with each one. Circulate and listen, but avoid interfering unless you are asked for help.

> **In the Know:** St. Augustine /ˈɔɡə,stin/ (354–430) was an early leader and thinker. He was born in what is now Algeria.
>
> Lin Yutang /lɪn yuˈtæŋ/ (1895–1976) was a Chinese writer and philosopher.
>
> George Moore (1873–1958) was a philosopher, born in London.
>
> Izaak Walton /ˈaɪzɪk ˈwɔltn/ (1593–1683) was an English writer.

b • Bring the class together to compare their ideas about the quotes. Have a show of hands to see how many people consider themselves "travelers" and how many prefer to stay at home.

3 ▶ Listening

a • Look at the pictures. Ask students *What is this man doing? (Asking for a ride. / Hitchhiking.) What is the woman doing? (She's traveling by train.)*

> **In the Know:** *Winnipeg* is the capital of Manitoba province in Central Canada.
>
> The word *hitchhike* /ˈhɪtʃhaɪk/ means to travel around by getting rides in other people's cars or trucks. People who hitchhike usually stand by the side of the road and signal to drivers with their thumb.

- Tell students that they are going to listen to four people talking about travel experiences. They should check the good or bad column and write where the experience happened.
- **AUDIO** Look at the example and play the recording of speaker 1. Check that students understand what to do.
- **AUDIO** Play the recording for the other speakers. Pause briefly after each speaker to give students time to write. Students could compare answers with a partner before the follow-up activity.
- Follow up by asking random students for their answers and what told them the experience was good or bad. Point out that the pronunciation of *Czech* is the same as that of the word *check*.

AK 2 *Good / Ireland*
3 *Good / California*
4 *Bad / Czech Republic*

b • Read the phrases and ask students if they can connect any of them to the stories. Accept any ideas.
- **AUDIO** Play the recording again straight through. Ask students to listen again to check their earlier ideas and complete the ones they did not remember. Tell students to write only the number of the story and key words while they are listening.
- **AUDIO** Make sure they don't try to write whole sentences while listening. Tell them they will have time to write sentences after the recording. Play the recording again if students are having difficulty.
- Give students time to write sentences from their notes. They could compare with a partner before the follow-up.
- Follow up by asking random students for the story and their explanation.
- **AUDIO** If there is any doubt or disagreement, play the recording again, stopping after each speaker for students to check. The key elements for each explanation are given below. Students' wording may vary.

AK 2 *Story 3–It was absolutely freezing.*
3 *Story 1–His passport was stolen from a mail truck.*
4 *Story 2–They saw a poem on the wall of a restaurant and loved it. Then someone introduced them to the poet.*
5 *Story 1–He had to cancel his trip because his passport was stolen.*
6 *Story 3–The man who stopped took them to his house and gave them a hot meal.*
7 *Story 4–The trip to Prague took six hours because they didn't change trains at the right time.*

c • Put students in pairs to choose one of the stories and retell it in their own words.

• Then tell students to find people who chose different stories. Ideally, they would work in groups of four, one for each story, but that will depend on how many students chose the same story.

• While they are retelling their stories, circulate and listen, but don't interfere unless you are asked for help. You could note common problems and discuss these at the end of the activity.

4 Vocabulary: Travel expressions

a • Have students read the list of expressions silently.

• **AUDIO** Tell them to listen to the stories in Section 3 again and circle the words and expressions they hear. Play the recording straight through.

• Follow up by asking students for the expressions they heard and in which story they came.

AK *(Numbers in parentheses refer to the stories.)*
to go on a (business) trip (1)   passport (1)   visa (1)
to take pictures (2)   to go sightseeing (2)
to buy a ticket (4)   train conductor (4)

b • Tell students to copy the chart into their notebooks and put the words and phrases into an appropriate column. Let students know that there may be more than one option for some items.

AK   *Possible answers:*

General Travel	Hotels and accommodation	Transportation
to go on a (business) trip	to make a reservation	one-way or round-trip ticket
passport	lobby	to reserve a seat
traveler's checks	single or double room	to take off
visa	to check in and out*	to land
to pack a suitcase	reception desk	to buy a ticket
to take pictures		window or aisle seat
to read a map		train conductor
to go sightseeing		hand luggage or carry-on bag
to get lost		ticket counter

Language Note: The expression *to check in** could go under Transportation *(check in for a flight)*, but not *check out*.

c • Put students into pairs or small groups to compare and discuss their answers.

• Follow up by asking if there were any differences and, if so, what they were.

5 ▸ In Conversation

• Look at the picture. Have students describe the situation and say, for example, what the people are doing or where they are. Then ask *What's the problem?* Accept any suggestions.

• **AUDIO** Ask students to cover the text and listen to check their ideas about the problem. Play the recording.

• **AUDIO** Play the recording again while students read the conversation and check their answers.

AK   *Angela and Henry are lost.*

6 Focus on Grammar

a • Have students look at the chart and answer the questions.

> **AK** 1 *The present perfect continuous is used for actions continuing up to the present (especially when we say how long the action has lasted).*
> 2 *The present perfect continuous is formed with* has / have + been + *the -ing form of the main verb.*

b • Have students underline two more examples of the present perfect continuous in the conversation.

> **AK** *...we've been walking...*　　　　*...I've been looking...*

> **Optional Activity:** Play the recording again and have students repeat the phrases with the present perfect continuous, paying attention to the pronunciation of the weak form of *been* /bɪn/ in these phrases.

c • Have students complete the paragraphs with the correct verbs in the present perfect continuous. Make sure students see that there is a separate list of verbs for each paragraph.

• Students could compare with a partner before the follow-up.

> **AK** 2 *We've been doing...*　　　3 *I've been trying...*
> 4 *...has been reading...*　　　5 *I've been working...*
> 6 *...I've been getting...*　　　7 *I've been finishing...*
> 8 *I haven't been sleeping...*

• Practice saying these phrases with the students. Also practice the question *What have you been doing lately?*, concentrating on the weak forms.

d • Put students in pairs to ask and answer the question *What have you been doing lately?* Encourage students to ask questions and add details to their answers

• Circulate and listen. Help with the pronunciation when necessary.

• Follow up by asking random students to say one thing about what their partner has / hasn't been doing lately.

7 ▶ Language in Action: Travel arrangements

a • Look at the pictures and have students describe each one and say what they think the people are doing. Accept any suggestions.

• Tell students they are going to listen to the conversations. They should check their ideas and say what change each person makes.

• **AUDIO** Play the recording of the first conversation. Ask students for their answers.

• **AUDIO** Repeat the sequence with the second conversation.

> **AK** 1 *The man is checking into the hotel. He changes the type of room, from a single to a double.*
> 2 *The person is at an airline ticket desk. He changes the day of the flight, from May 11 to June 1.*

b • Give students time to read the phrases in the chart silently.

• **AUDIO** Tell them to listen and number the phrases in the order they hear them. Play the recording straight through.

• **AUDIO** Follow up by asking random students for the order. If there is any doubt or disagreement, play the recording again, pausing after each phrase for students to check.

AK

Hotel Reception	Airline Ticket Counter
3 Can you fill out this form, please?	5 Here's your new ticket.
2 How many nights are you staying?	3 When would you like to fly?
5 Here are your keys.	1 Is it possible to change my flight?
1 I have a reservation.	4 There's a flight at (time) on (date).
4 Can I have your credit card, please?	2 There's a (amount) charge to change this ticket.

c • Look at the flow chart with the students to make sure they understand how it works.

• Put students in pairs to practice the conversations. Tell them to use their own information and choose what they want to change.

• Ask students to change roles and practice again.

- Follow up by asking some pairs to repeat one of their conversations for the group.

> **Optional Activity:** Large-scale hotel role-play. Divide the class into two groups. One group should be at least twice the size of the other group. Students in Group A (the smaller group) are hotel receptionists. Those in Group B are travelers. Give Group B small pieces of paper and ask them to write their name, how long they are staying, and what kind of room they want, but tell them that at least one piece of information should be incorrect. Meanwhile, tell Group A to organize their reception desk and make a plan of the rooms in the hotel (how many are single, how many double, etc.)
>
> Collect the pieces of paper from Group B and give them to Group A to assign rooms. When everything is ready, announce that a bus from the airport has just arrived at the hotel and get all the "travelers" to arrive at once. Tell the travelers to get in line and "check in." Each traveler announces his / her name and the receptionist finds the reservation, checks it with the traveler, makes appropriate changes, and ends the conversation politely.
>
> While "waiting" in line, students could converse in English, for example, about their trips or how they feel about waiting so long.

8 Writing

a • Tell students they are going to write a short account of something that happened during a trip. These will be "published" for everyone to read in a class book or displayed around the room.

- Explain that professional writers work with an editor who asks questions and makes suggestions to make the writing clearer or more interesting. When this has been done, a proofreader looks at the writing and corrects the language and punctuation. Tell them they are going to work as writers, editors, and proofreaders at different stages of this activity.

- Have students think about when and where they travel. This could be a long trip or a routine journey, such as visiting relatives or even going to work.

- Tell them the paragraph can be about something good, bad, or funny.

- Ask them to think about where they were going, what preparations they made, and what happened.

- Give students three or four minutes to make notes before they start writing their paragraphs.

- Give students time, not more than fifteen minutes, to write their paragraphs.

b • Let students choose a partner to work with. They will be each other's
       editors.

   • They should each read the other's story and ask questions for clarification
     and more detail. They should look at the **content** of the story.

   • Have students rewrite their stories, including the extra points and details.

   • Then students could act as proofreaders. Have them exchange stories
     again, look at the language, and make suggestions for corrections. If
     necessary, have students rewrite the stories.

   • The final versions of the stories should be displayed. You could put
     the stories up around the room and invite the class to circulate and
     read them.

   • **Option:** Instead of posting the stories around the room, you could
     paste them into a large-format notebook. Some students might like to
     contribute photos or other forms of illustrations to the book.

9 Reading

a • The first reading should be done very quickly. The students should look
       for the relevant information, rather than reading every word.

   • Have students read part A (the book review) quickly and answer the
     questions.

   • Follow up by asking random students for their answers and the reasons
     for them.

     AK *It's an adventure at sea—a boat trip.*
             The review is positive ("highly recommended").

b • Have students read the review again more slowly and answer the
       questions. It isn't necessary for students to include all the details noted
       below. Their answers should show that they understand the "gist" of
       the text.

     AK *Possible answers:*
             1 *He joined the group by chance. He met one of the crew members*
               while traveling in Bolivia. At first he only wanted to write about
               the trip.
             2 *They were inexperienced. They "had very little sailing experience.*
               They couldn't even turn the boat around."

c • Have students look at the pictures to find out other information about the voyage.

 • Make sure students understand the parts of the boat labeled in one of the pictures.

d • Tell students to read section B very quickly to answer the question *What kind of situation are they in?* Accept any reasonable response to this question.

> *AK*   *Possible answers:*
> *They're in an emergency situation. There's a storm; it's raining. They're afraid the boat might sink.*

> **In the Know:** A *life jacket* is a jacket with pockets often filled with air that helps people to float if they fall into water. A *safety harness* has straps that go round the body and that can be attached to a rope fixed to the boat. The *waterline* on a boat is the line that marks the height that the water reaches on the side of a boat.

e • Have students read section B again more slowly to answer the questions.

 • Follow up by asking random students for their answers and reasons. Accept any reasonable response. Answers below indicate the most important points.

> *AK*   *Possible answers:*
> 1 *He heard a muffled roar.*
> 2 *It was raining.*
> 3 *He said, "Everybody up! We have an emergency!"*
> 4 *The boat was a mess. The sails were on the wrong side of the mast. The boat had already sunk a foot lower than when they left. It could be sinking.*
> 5 *He thought the boat might sink.*

f • Have students look at the text and list the vocabulary related to the three topics.

 • Students could compare their lists with a partner before the follow-up.

 • Follow up by writing the three topics on the board and asking random students to add words to the lists. Clarify the meanings as necessary.

AK *Possible answers:*
The boat and equipment: *cabin, life jacket, safety harness, safety rope, sails, mast, reeds, waterline*
The weather: *torrential rain*
People's feelings: *sleepy, anxious, fear, tight, relaxed*

g • Either have a quick class discussion or put students in small groups to share their opinions.

10 Vocabulary: Prepositions and nouns

a • Have students read the sentences and add the examples to the diagrams.

AK by: *hand / chance / bus / e-mail / satellite phone*
on: *the radio*
in: *Bolivia / touch / the newspaper*

b • Put students in pairs. Tell them to study the diagrams together and then cover the words and try to remember the prepositions and the nouns.

• Follow up by asking if students think this way of memorizing could be used for other vocabulary groups.

11 Listening

a • Ask students the questions. Brainstorm what the difficulties of early exploration were.

• Ask what early explorers students know about.

b • Tell students they are going to listen to an interview with Annelise /ˈænəlɪs/ Morgan, a woman who enjoys adventure, travel, and exploration.

• Tell students to listen and answer the questions *Does Annelise believe modern exploration is more or less difficult than early exploration? (Less difficult.)* and *Does she believe people will continue to explore? (Yes.)*

• **AUDIO** Play the recording straight through.

• Follow up by asking random students for their answers and reasons.

c • **AUDIO** Read through the questions with the students. Accept any ideas they have for the answers, but don't confirm or deny them. Play the recording again for them to listen and check or complete their answers.

- Follow up by asking random students for their answers and the reasons for them. Sometimes it may be useful to elicit information from several students in order to get a complete response. For example, see question 4 in which students might come up with several examples.

- **AUDIO** If there is any doubt or disagreement, play the recording again, pausing at appropriate points for the students to check.

> **AK**   *Possible answers:*
> 1 *She has climbed mountains, sailed across an ocean, and walked across deserts.*
> 2 *When she was a kid, she read a lot about explorers.*
> 3 *There weren't many. It was not easy for them. Some of them even used to wear men's clothing to disguise themselves.*
> 4 *They had no high-tech equipment and almost no safety equipment. They had no lightweight clothing or equipment. They wore heavy clothes and carried heavy equipment. Their transport was slow.*

d • Ask students *What modern explorers do you know of?*

- Have a quick class discussion.

> **Optional Activity:** If your students are very interested in this subject, some of them might like to do some research about explorers and present their results to the group in a later class.

12 ▸ Focus on Grammar

a • Look at the chart. Have students circle the correct answer in item 1 and answer the question in item 2.

> **AK**   1 Used to *describes situations, regular actions, or routines in the past.*
> 2 *Questions and negatives are formed with the auxiliary* did *(negative* did not / didn't*).*

> **Language Note:** *Used to* refers to a situation, habit, or state that was true in the past. This situation, habit, or state has usually changed, and the present situation, habit, or state is different. There is no present form.

- Make sure students notice that in the negative and question forms, the base form *use* occurs after the auxiliary *did*.

> **Language Note:** The verb *use* in the expression *used to* is pronounced with an unvoiced /s/ sound (/yustə/). When this word occurs with the meaning of *utilize*, it is pronounced with a voiced /z/ sound (/yuzd/). Notice the difference in the pronunciation of the word *used* in these sentences. *He used* /yuzd/ *wood to make the guitar. They used to* /yustə/ *make boats with reeds.*

b • Go over the example sentence with the students.

• Have students complete items 2–4 and then compare their responses with a partner.

> **AK** 2 *They didn't use to travel by plane.*
> 3 *Women used to wear long dresses.*
> 4 *Trips used to take much longer.*

c • Have students write sentences using the suggested categories. Put students in small groups to compare their sentences.

• Follow up by asking each group for the most interesting or surprising sentence.

13 ▶ *KnowHow*: Improving fluency

a • Either have a class discussion or put students in pairs or small groups to read the definition of *fluency* and discuss the questions.

• Follow up by asking for the most general opinions in the groups. If students need some ideas to get the discussion going, ask a couple of "starter" questions. For example, *Is it easier to speak to just one other person or to speak in a larger group? Do you feel more comfortable speaking to someone you know or to a stranger, for example, a salesperson? What kinds of topics or situations are difficult for you when speaking English?*

b • Ask students to work together to decide which strategies might be most useful in each situation. If necessary, get the discussion going by asking students something like *When is it possible to plan what you want to say beforehand?* (Students might respond, for example, that it is difficult to plan for a party where conversation tends to be fast and spontaneous. But you can plan for a presentation or introducing yourself.)

• Follow up by asking each group for their opinions.

c • Remind students to use some of these strategies in the next section.

14 Speaking

a • Tell students that they are going to role-play travel agents to create an interesting vacation and prepare a presentation to advertise it.

• Tell students to use the questions to help them with their presentation. Read through the questions with the students and elicit one or two examples to get them started.

• Put students in small groups to create their presentation. Give students time to make notes for their presentation.

b • Tell students that each group is going to present their trip and that each student should choose one trip that they would like to take.

• Remind them to use some of the strategies suggested in section 13.

• Have each group present their trip to the whole class.

• **Option:** Make new groups in which each group contains one representative from each of the previous groups. The representatives present their trips to the new group. One way to do this quickly is to assign each student in a group a different number or letter, for example, 1, 2, 3, 4. Then have all the 1s form a new group, and do the same with the 2s, 3s, and 4s.

Note: If your class is very big, the "option" would be better as more students are involved at any one time.

• Follow up by having a show of hands for each trip. Is there a trip that is the most popular?

• Ask students which strategies from section 13 they used, and if they found any strategies especially helpful.

> **Optional Activity:** For additional written work, you could ask students to produce a brochure for the trip they presented.

Units 7–9 Review

Grammar

1 *Possible answer:*
The farmer found an old wooden table. He will sell the table because his family needs the money.

2 2 *I am* 3 *isn't he* 4 *he is*
5 *did you* 6 *I didn't* 7 *did we*

3 2 *'m (am) going to*
3 *'s (is) going to*
4 *'ll (will)*

4 2 *In Latin America, corn is often made into flour for tortillas and other dishes.*
3 *In the past apples and pears were grown in Harold's area, but now wheat is grown.*
4 *The cakes were made (by the bakery) for the party two days ago.*
OR The cakes for the party were made (by the bakery) two days ago.

5 1 *a few* 2 *tomatoes* 3 *The tomatoes*
4 *a little* 5 *Corn*

6 2 *have ('ve) been sitting* 3 *have you been doing*
4 *have not (haven't) been doing* 5 *have ('ve) just been looking*
6 *have ('ve) been thinking*

7 2 *used to go* 3 *used to enjoy* 4 *did not (didn't) use to bother*
Possible questions:
Where did the writer use to go very often?
What did the writer use to enjoy?
What didn't use to bother the writer?

Vocabulary

8 1 *lend* 2 *by* 3 *reservation* 4 *experience* 5 *on*

Recycling Center

9 2 *met* 3 *were* 4 *have ('ve) been* 5 *came*
6 *did not (didn't) know* 7 *was* 8 *has been*

Fun Spot

horizontal words: steam, peel (spelled backwards), mix, boil
vertical words: fry (spelled backwards), grill, roast

10 *Hard to believe?*

Main aims of this unit

Grammar: First conditional; advisability: Modals and expressions

Vocabulary: Easily confused verbs; phrasal verbs

Functions: Saying what you believe or don't believe

Unit Overview

Listening:	News story about sports and superstitions
Vocabulary:	Easily confused verbs
Focus on Grammar:	First conditional
Language in Action:	Saying what you believe or don't believe
Writing and Speaking:	Your own superstitions
Listening:	Song
KnowHow:	Common vowel sounds
Reading:	Reading Faces
In Conversation:	"I think I'd better get a new suit."
Focus on Grammar:	Advisability: Modals and expressions
Listening:	Stories of first impressions
Vocabulary:	Phrasal verbs
Speaking and Writing:	Personal stories of first impressions

Warm-up

Ask students about objects or actions that are linked with good or bad luck. For example, seeing a black cat is considered lucky in Britain, but bad luck in the United States. In some parts of the world, people say that breaking a mirror will bring seven years of bad luck.

1 ▶ Listening

a • Put students in pairs to list as many sports as they can in one minute.

   • Compare lists as a whole class.

   • Look at the photos and have students say what they know about these sports.

b • Tell students they are going to listen to part of a radio program about superstitions in sports.

   • They should listen and number the sports in the pictures in the order they are mentioned, and try to hear what the significance of a coin is.

   • **AUDIO** Play the recording straight through.

   • Follow up by asking individual students for answers.

> **AK**   rodeo riding: 3
> ice hockey: 1
> baseball: 2
> golf: 4
> People say that the Canadian coin buried under the ice in the last Olympics brought the Canadians good luck. They won two gold medals. The coin is being taken to the Hockey Hall of Fame.

> **In the Know:** *Hall of Fame:* A Hall of Fame is a sort of museum dedicated to a sport or activity, for example, the Baseball Hall of Fame or the Rock and Roll Hall of Fame. Visitors to a Hall of Fame can see all kinds of memorabilia related to the sport or activity. It is an honor for someone to be made a member of a Hall of Fame.
>
> *Ice keeper:* Ice hockey is played on an ice rink. It is very important for the ice to be as smooth and clean as possible for the skaters. The ice keeper's job is to maintain the ice in good condition.

c • **AUDIO** Read the list. Tell students to listen again and say which sport these things are associated with and whether they are supposed to be good or bad luck. Play the recording straight through again.

• **AUDIO** Follow up by asking random students for answers. If there is any doubt or disagreement, play the recording again, pausing at appropriate points for the students to check.

> *AK* 2 *baseball—good luck*
> 3 *baseball—bad luck*
> 4 *rodeo riding—bad luck*
> 5 *rodeo riding—bad luck*
> 6 *rodeo riding—bad luck / golf—good luck*

d • Either have a class discussion or put students in small groups to discuss the questions.

• If students worked in groups, follow up by asking each group to summarize their discussion.

2 Vocabulary: Easily confused verbs

a • Put students in pairs to answer the questions.

• Follow up by asking random pairs for answers.

> *AK* 1 *You <u>wear</u> clothes, <u>carry</u> a bag, and <u>use</u> a computer.*
> 2 *You <u>bring</u> something towards you and you <u>take</u> something away from you.*
> 3 *You <u>win</u> a race or competition and <u>earn</u> money for working.*
> 4 *You <u>miss</u> a ball, a bus, a class, etc. If you can't find something, you <u>lose</u> it.*
> 5 *You <u>watch</u> something which is changing or developing (for example, TV, a sporting event, etc.). You <u>look at</u> something static (a picture, a book, etc.).*
> 6 *You <u>meet</u> someone for the first time. You <u>know</u> people you have already met.*

b • Have students circle the correct verb.

> *AK* 1 *wear*   2 *met*   3 *earn*
> 4 *miss*   5 *take*   6 *watch*

• Follow up by asking random students for answers.

> **Optional Activity:** Ask students to write similar sentences of their own in their notebooks to give them a personalized record.

3 ▶ Focus on Grammar

a • Have students look at the chart and answer the questions.

> **AK** 1 *simple present*
> 2 *Yes, you can change the order of clauses in a conditional sentence. You use a comma when the* if *clause comes first.*

Note: First conditionals are used to express possible real conditions. The condition proposed in the *if* clause may or may not happen. The main clause proposes the result. For example, *If I take the train (possible real condition), I'll be late (result).*

> **In the Know:** *Sports words. Tennis*—In tennis the *court lines* are the lines that mark the boundaries of the playing area. *Serving* the ball means to put the ball into play for the other player(s) to try to return it.
> *Bowling*—This is a popular sport in the United States. In this game, the players roll a large, heavy ball down a long wooden lane toward a group of ten pins. They try to knock down as many pins as they can.

• **Help Desk:** Emphasize the use of the simple present in the *if* clause.

b • Look at the prompts and the example sentence and make sure students understand that the *if* clause does not always come first.

• Have students write sentences from the other prompts.

• Follow up by asking random students for a sentence. Ask whether the sentence has a comma between the clauses or not.

> **AK** 2 *You won't have good luck if you step on the court lines.*
> 3 *If you wear the same clothes, you'll continue winning.*
> 4 *If you wear double numbers on your uniform, you'll have good luck.*
> 5 *If you hold more than two balls when serving, you won't serve well.*
> 6 *You will have a good game if you wipe the bottoms of your shoes.*

c • Look at the example sentence. Work as a class or in small groups to explain other superstitions.

• Give students the model *In (sport, etc.) if you..., you will / won't....*

• You could get students to write the sentences on the board.

d • Look at the example of a sentence chain.

• Put students in small groups to make other sentence chains, starting with the prompts given.

- Circulate and listen. Check that students are practicing the structure correctly.

- If they are making a lot of mistakes, stop the activity and practice some more chains as a choral drill. For example, give the prompt *If it rains tomorrow / go to the park / stay at home / watch TV / not study,* etc. Then go back to the small groups.

- Follow up by asking how long the groups managed to keep going.

> **Optional Activity:** First conditional consequences. Based on an old party game, this should be done fast and light-heartedly. Give each student a long, narrow piece of paper. Ask students to think of a sentence with an *if* clause. Have students write the *if* clause at the top of the paper and then fold the paper over so the *if* clause can't be seen. Students should then hand the paper to the person on his or her left. The next student should write the second part of the sentence on the piece of paper they received (without looking at the *if* clause) and fold it over again. Hand the paper to the person on the left and write another *if* clause on the paper they received, fold it over, etc. Do this as many times as the students can. Then open the papers and read the sentences. Ask students to read out the funniest, the most illogical, or the one they liked best.

4 ▸ Language in Action: Saying what you believe or don't believe

a • Look at the pictures. Have students describe the situation and say what they think the "parking tiger" does. Accept any suggestions.

- **AUDIO** Tell students to listen to the conversation and say what the "parking tiger" does, according to Michele /mɪˈʃɛl/. Play the recording straight through.

- Follow up by asking what Michele says the parking tiger does.

> **AK** *She says that when she presses the button, the head moves and she will find a parking space soon.*

b • Go over the expressions in the chart with the class.

- **AUDIO** Tell students to listen again and check the expressions they hear in the conversation. Play the recording again.

- Follow up by asking random students for the expressions they checked.

> **AK** ✓ *I really believe (that)… /* ✓ *I always think (that)… /* ✓ *It (really) works. /* ✓ *Oh, come on! /* ✓ *That's too much!*

c • You could practice the expressions, especially the intonation before starting this activity.

  • Look at the example conversation. Put students in pairs to make their own conversations, using the suggestions or their own ideas. Encourage them to keep the conversation going.

  • Circulate and listen, but don't interfere unless you are asked to help. Follow up by asking some pairs to repeat their conversations for the group.

5 ▶ Writing and Speaking

a • Tell students to think about any superstition they have. Tell them they are going to write a short description of their superstition or write why they don't have any.

  • Go over the example. Give students a few minutes to write on a separate piece of paper. Make sure they don't put their names on the papers.

  • Collect the papers. Number each description.

b • Put students in small groups.

  • Read out the first description and tell the groups to discuss who they think it belongs to. Tell them to write the name down. Then read out number two and so on until you have read out all the descriptions.

  • If the class is too big for you to read all the descriptions, give each group a random collection of descriptions to read and discuss.

  • Follow up by asking who each description belongs to.

  • **Option:** Put all the descriptions up around the room. Put students in pairs to circulate and decide together who they think each one belongs to.

6 ▶ Listening: Song

a • Ask students to cover the song or close their books.

  • **AUDIO** Play the recording. Students should listen and answer the questions *What is the magic the singer believes in? What causes it?*

> **In the Know:** Song lyrics often do not use standard spelling and punctuation. Commas, periods, and question marks are often used inconsistently in song lyrics. For example, in the case of the song *Do You Believe in Magic*, there is no question mark in the title.

  • Ask students for their ideas. Then ask them to read the words of the song and check their ideas.

AK *The singer believes in the magic in a young girl's heart. Music causes this magic.*

b • Have students find the words from the list in the song and circle them.

• Ask students to copy the chart into their notebook and check that they know the sounds of the phonetic symbols: (/i/) (/ɪ/) (/eɪ/) (/ɛ/).

Pronunciation Note: The sounds /i/ and /eɪ/ are often referred to as long sounds. The length of the sound distinguishes them from the short sounds /ɪ/ and /ɛ/. Contrast the words *feet* /fit/ and *fit* /fɪt/. Notice how the vowel sound of *feet* seems to go on longer than that in *fit*. The same is true of the sounds /eɪ/ and /ɛ/, as in *late* /leɪt/ and *let* /lɛt/. In English /eɪ/ is actually a diphthong, as the /e/ resolves into an /ɪ/ at the end. This may help students as they listen for and practice saying these words.

• **AUDIO** Play the song again. Tell students to listen and put the words in the correct columns, according to the sound of the underlined vowel(s).

• You could copy the chart on to the board and ask random students to write the words in the correct column on the board.

• Practice saying the words in each column. Then practice the words in random order.

AK /i/ *feet / seem / free*
/ɪ/ *magic / rhythm / listen*
/eɪ/ *face / late / maybe*
/ɛ/ *then / set*

Optional Activity: You could play the song again so that the students can sing along with it. Ask them to pay particular attention to the sounds of the vowels above.

7 ▷ *KnowHow*: Common vowel sounds

a • **AUDIO** Have students look at the pairs of words and listen to the recording. You could have students repeat after each pair.

• If necessary, exaggerate the difference between the long and short sounds. You could use your hands to indicate the length of the long sounds.

• Then go back to the natural pronunciation and have students repeat.

b • **AUDIO** Tell students they are going to hear one word from each pair. They should underline the word they hear. Play the recording.

• **AUDIO** If necessary, play the recording again.

• Follow up by asking random students for the word they heard. Ask *How do you spell it?* to check they are correct.

> **AK** 1 *feet*   2 *live*   3 *fill*   4 *sheep*
> 5 *let*   6 *tale*   7 *gate*   8 *test*

c • Put students in pairs to practice. Have one student say one word from each pair in 7b. The other student circles or writes the word he or she hears. Then have students check to see if the answers are correct. Students should then switch roles and repeat the activity.

• Circulate and listen to the pronunciation.

8 ▶ Reading

a • Discuss the three photos of people smiling with the class. Ask *What differences do you see? How would you interpret the smiles? Do all the smiles indicate happiness? Are they all sincere?*

b • Give students one minute to skim the article *Reading Faces* and decide which sentence, *a* or *b*, provides the best summary.

• Follow up by asking random students for their answers and the reasons for it.

> **AK** b *(The first part of the article talks about facial expressions. The third paragraph mentions the shape of the face.)*

c • Read the statements with the students. If they can answer any of them, accept their ideas but ask them to read again to check.

• Have students read the article again, more slowly and write *T* (true), *F* (false), or *NI* (no information) for each statement.

• Have students compare their answers with a partner before the follow-up.

• Follow up by asking random students for their answers and the evidence for it.

> **AK** 1 *T*   2 *T*   3 *F*   4 *NI*   5 *T*   6 *F*   7 *NI*

d • Have students find the words in the article and choose the correct definition.

• Remind students to read the whole sentence before deciding.

- Follow up by asking random students for their answers and how they decided.

  AK 2 *f*   3 *e*   4 *c*   5 *a*   6 *h*   7 *d*   8 *b*

e • Either have a class discussion or put students in groups to exchange ideas.

9 In Conversation

- Ask students to cover the conversation or close their books.

- **AUDIO** Tell them to listen to the conversation and answer the questions *What are Martin and Rita talking about? Do they agree?* Play the recording straight through.

- Ask students for their ideas. Don't accept or reject their suggestions at this time.

- **AUDIO** Tell students to read the conversation and check their answers. Play the recording again while they are reading.

  AK *Possible answer:*
  Martin and Rita are talking about buying a new suit for a job interview. Martin thinks it will make a better first impression. Rita disagrees with him; she doesn't think they will judge him on his clothes.

10 Focus on Grammar

a • Tell students to look at the chart and answer the questions *Which expressions use* to? *Which don't? How is the negative formed for each one?*

  AK 1 *The expressions* ought to *and* supposed to *use* to. *The expressions* had better *and* should *don't.*
  2 *shouldn't / had better not / (am / are / is) not supposed to*

> **Pronunciation Note:** When *ought to* occurs in the middle of a sentence, the two words usually run together and sound like /ˈɔtə/. For example, *He ought to* /ˈɔtə/ *buy a suit*. When *ought to* occurs at the end of a sentence, it is pronounced /ˈɔt tu/. For example, *Should he buy a suit?—Yes, I think he ought to.* /ˈɔt tu/

> **Language Note:** Students may be confused by the use of the past form *had* to refer to future recommendations in the expression *had better....* There is no simple explanation for this, and students should just treat it as an expression. Historically, the origin of this usage is similar to the use of the past tense in the *if* clause in second conditional sentences where it is used to express present unreal conditions. *Had better...* means *it would be better if....*

- Have students look back at the conversation in section 9 to find more examples of the expressions in the chart.

- Make sure students understand the note about *ought to* and *had better* in negatives and questions.

b • Go over the example with the class. Make sure that students see that the expressions of advisability are paired with verbs on the list. This should give them clues as to which expression they should use in each case. In the example, the person states a problem and asks for advice. Therefore, *What should I do?* is the correct response.

- Tell students to fill in the blanks using the words and expressions from the list.

- Remind students to read the whole sentence in order to choose which expression to use.

- They could compare with a partner before the follow-up.

- Follow up by asking random students for their responses.

> **AK** 2 ...*are not supposed to park...*
> 3 ...*ought to try...*
> 4 ...*had better not touch...*
> 5 ...*is supposed to start...*
> 6 ...*had better see...*

c • Read through the situations with the students. Let them suggest some advice if they want to.

- Give students time to write their advice to their friends in the situations. Tell them to refer to section 10a to make sure they use the most appropriate advisability modal.

- Put students in pairs to compare and discuss their advice. Encourage them to keep the conversations going by using questions and explanations.

- Circulate and listen. Follow up by asking how many pairs agreed with each other's advice.

11 ▶ Listening

a • Look at the pictures and ask students to describe the situations and what is happening in each one.

• Make sure students understand *a flat tire* and *a flat*.

• You could ask students for their impressions of the people in the pictures, using *She / He looks… They look… (+ adjectives)*.

• **AUDIO** Tell students to listen to the two stories and say what was not true in each case. Play the recording, stopping after each story to give students time to think about what they have heard. Make sure students are focusing on listening at this point and not trying to take notes.

• **AUDIO** Follow up by asking random students for their answers. If necessary, play the recording again.

> **AK** 1 *He thought the new boss wasn't very nice.*
> 2 *They thought the men on the motorcycles were scary and dangerous.*

b • Read through the pieces of information with the students. Tell them to listen again and write 1 or 2 beside each item, depending on which story it goes with.

• Follow up by asking random students which story each piece of information goes with and what the significance of each point is.

• **AUDIO** If there is any doubt or disagreement, play the recording again, pausing between the two stories.

AK

Story 1	Story 2
a new boss	a flat tire
she wasn't very friendly	a gang of men
dropped files and spilled coffee	"Give me your keys"
she started laughing	changed the tire
more responsibility	"Go home"
a good friend now	

c • Either have a class discussion or put students in small groups. You could suggest they think about what their own reactions would be in the situations described.

12 Vocabulary: Phrasal verbs

a • Look at the phrasal verbs. Review the phrasal verbs and definitions in the glossary.

• **AUDIO** Have students listen to the stories from section 11 again and mark the phrasal verbs they hear.

• **AUDIO** Play the recording of Story 1 and check with the students.

• **AUDIO** Then play the recording of Story 2 and check.

> **AK** Story 1: *take over*   *pick up*   *sit down*   *take on*
> Story 2: *pull over*   *get out of*   *get on*   *get off*   *give back*

b • Tell students to rewrite the sentences in their notebooks, replacing the underlined words with the correct form of a phrasal verb.

• Follow up by asking random students for their answers.

> **AK** 2 *Monica didn't want to get off the bus…*
> 3 *Can you give back my CD, please? OR*
>   *Can you give my CD back, please?*
> 4 *…so we pulled over.*
> 5 *A new company is taking over ours. OR*
>   *A new company is taking ours over.*

> **Language Note:** There are both separable and inseparable phrasal verbs in section 12. The separable verbs are *take over, pick up, take on, pull over,* and *give back*. The inseparable verbs are *sit down, stand up, get in / into, get out of,* and *get off*. This would also be a good time to remind students that *get out of* is usually used to describe leaving a car. With a bus, plane, ship, bicycle, or motorcycle, *get off* is used.

c • Put students in pairs to retell the stories using as many phrasal verbs as they can.

• Circulate and listen.

13 Speaking and Writing

a • Give students a moment to think about a situation which involved first impressions. Read the questions in a calm voice while they are thinking.

• Put students in pairs to tell each other about the situation. Encourage students to ask follow-up questions, asking for clarification or more detail and reasons.

- Circulate and listen, but avoid interfering unless you are asked for help.

b - Have students write paragraphs about their examples. Remind them to include the extra details that their partner asked about.

- This could be assigned for homework.

- When students have finished, ask them to proofread their own paragraph and correct any mistakes they find.

c - Put students in small groups to compare their stories and discuss the questions.

- Follow up by asking each group for their conclusions.

11 *Down to earth*

Main aims of this unit

Grammar: Modals: Possibility (speculation); reported requests with *ask, tell,* and *want*

Vocabulary: Geography; prepositions of movement

Functions: Directions

Unit Overview

Speaking:	Comparing landscapes
Vocabulary:	Geography
Listening:	Health benefits of nature
Focus on Grammar:	Modals: Possibility (speculation)
Reading:	An article about an oceanographer
Vocabulary:	Prepositions of movement
Language in Action:	Directions
Listening:	Animal intelligence
Writing:	A story about a special characteristic of an animal
In Conversation:	"She told me not to worry about that."
Focus on Grammar:	Reported requests with *ask, tell,* and *want*
KnowHow:	Choosing vocabulary to learn
Speaking:	Choosing an appropriate pet

Warm-up

Ask students about the area where they live. For example, *Are there a lot of plants near where you live? Is the area in general very green? Do you like to go to parks or to the country?*

1 Speaking

a • Put students in pairs to look at the pictures and tell each other which scenes they like the most and the least. Have students explain why.

b • As a whole class, compare answers. Ask random students which natural setting they liked the most. Then ask random students why they chose it.

• Ask random students which pictures they liked the least and why.

• Have a show of hands to decide if there is a natural setting most people prefer.

2 Vocabulary: Geography

a • Have students look at the photos in section 1 and identify as many natural features as possible. Don't confirm or deny any answers.

• Have students read the vocabulary words in 2a. Ask them to find the corresponding numbers in the photos to confirm their answers.

• Follow up by checking that students have correctly identified the natural features.

> **In the Know:** Students often ask about the difference between a *hill* and a *mountain*. There is no absolute dividing line. A hill is generally smaller than a mountain and may not have an identifiable peak. A mountain is usually taller, rockier, and more rugged.

b • ***Help Desk:*** Read through the examples with the students. Have students use these guidelines as they give specific examples in 2b.

> **Language Note:** Although *the* is used with the names of oceans, seas, and rivers, it is not usually used with lakes or waterfalls. For example, *the Atlantic Ocean* but *Lake Titicaca; the Niagara River* but *Niagara Falls*. It is important that students understand that there is no "rhyme or reason" for these differences. It is just a matter of custom.

- Students could work in pairs to give an example for each word. Ask them to write the lists in their notebooks.

- Follow up by asking random students and getting as many examples as possible from the class. Accept both local and international examples.

> AK *Some possible answers:*
> *Mountains: Mount Everest (Nepal, Tibet), Mont Blanc (the highest mountain in Europe), Cerro Aconcagua (the highest mountain in South America), Mount McKinley (the highest mountain in the U.S.)*
> *Mountain ranges: the Alps (Europe), the Rocky Mountains (U.S.)*
> *Forests: the Black Forest (Germany)*
> *Deserts: the Gobi Desert (Central Asia), the Kalahari Desert (Southern Africa)*
> *Rivers: the Amazon (Brazil), the Yangtze-Kiang (China), the Mississippi (U.S.)*
> *Lakes: Lake Superior (Canada, U.S.), Lake Victoria (Kenya, Tanzania, Uganda)*
> *Oceans: the Pacific Ocean, the Atlantic Ocean, the Indian Ocean, the Arctic Ocean*
> *Rainforests: the Amazon Forest (South America), the Ituri Forest (Zaire)*
> *Waterfalls: Niagara Falls (Canada, U.S.), Iguaçu Falls (Argentina, Brazil), Angel Falls (Venezuela)*
> *Islands: Greenland (the largest island in the world), Victoria Island (Canada)*

3 Listening

a • Have students describe the picture.

- **AUDIO** Look at the three possible topics and tell students they are going to listen to a conversation between three people who are in a garden. They should choose the main topic. Play the recording straight through.

- Check with the students what they thought the main topic was and why.

> AK 2 *Nature and health.*

b • Read the questions and allow students to suggest answers but don't accept or reject any ideas at this point.

- **AUDIO** Play the recording again. Ask students to listen again to check their ideas or find the answers.

- Follow up by asking students to discuss their answers and the reasons for them. It might help to make notes of key ideas on the board.

- **AUDIO** Play the recording again and stop at key points for students to verify their ideas. The answers below give the main ideas. Accept any responses that convey these ideas.

> **AK** 1 *He's doing research into how contact with nature might have positive health benefits.*
> 2 *He mentions that in one study patients in a hospital who had a view of trees stayed less time than those with a view of a brick wall. In another study, office employees reported that plants in the workplace made them feel calmer.*
> 3 *He always feels calmer after working in the garden.*

c • Either have a class discussion or put students in small groups.

- You could have students talk about their own experiences. Have they heard of any other reports in relation to nature and health? What do they think of the ideas in the conversation?

- If students worked in groups, follow up by asking each group to summarize their ideas for the class.

4 Focus on Grammar

> **Language Note:** This grammar section presents the use of modals to describe possibilities when a person is speculating about something by drawing logical conclusions on the basis of evidence or guessing.
>
> The modals *may, might,* and *could* can also be used for future possibility. For example, *He may take a history course next semester. He isn't sure yet.*
>
> Make sure students do not confuse *may be* with *maybe*. For example, *I may be there.* vs. *Maybe I'll be there.*

a • Have students look at the chart and answer the questions.

> **AK** 1 *may, might, could*   2 *can't*   3 *must*

b • Have students fill in the blanks with modal verbs. They should consider how sure the speakers are about what they are saying.

- Have students compare with a partner before the follow-up.

- Follow up by asking random students for the complete sentence and ask why they used the verb.

AK 1 *may* OR *might* OR *could (possible)*
 2 *can't (impossible)*
 3 *may* OR *might* OR *could (possible)* / *may* OR *might* OR *could (possible)*
 4 *can't (impossible)*
 5 *must (almost certain)*

c • Tell students to look at the painting and speculate about it using the modal verbs from the chart and vocabulary from section 2. They could do this in pairs or as a whole class.

• If they work in pairs, follow up by asking each pair for one of their sentences.

Optional Activity: Ask students to think about friends and members of their family. Put them in pairs. Have them tell their partner where these people *may, can't,* or *must be* at the moment and why they think that.

5 Reading

a • Have students look at the photograph and describe the things around Curtis Ebbesmeyer.

• Introduce the word *beachcomber*. Ask students if they can recognize the two words that make up this term. (Beach *and* comb. *As a verb,* comb *means to look through something thoroughly.*) Then ask what they think the word means.

In the Know: A *beachcomber* is a person who searches a beach for shells and other things. Some people do this in order to sell what they find. For this reason, the word is often associated with people who have an unconventional lifestyle.

• Have students read the introduction and speculate about the answer to the question. Remind them to use modal verbs from section 4. Don't accept or reject students' ideas at this time.

• It might be useful to make notes of students' ideas on the board to refer to later.

b • Tell students to skim the article to check their guesses from section 5a.

AK Possible answer:
They help Curtis Ebbesmeyer track the patterns of ocean currents.

c • Have students read the article again slowly to answer the questions.

• They could compare answers with a partner before the follow-up.

• Follow up by asking random students for their answers and the reason for their answers.

> *AK* 1 *His approach is old-fashioned. He doesn't use high-tech equipment.*
> 2 *He got started when he heard that shoes were washing up on the northwest shores of the United States.*
> 3 *He tracked the route across the ocean from where they fell into the water to where they landed.*
> 4 *Beachcombers give him information about objects that land on beaches all over the world.*
> 5 *The bathtub toys gave Ebbesmeyer a lot of new and accurate information (OR data) for his research.*
> 6 *The association has 500 members. They have documented information about spills.*

d • Either work as a class or put students in small groups to discuss the questions.

• If they worked in small groups, follow up by asking each group to summarize their discussion for the class.

6 Vocabulary: Prepositions of movement

a • Have students look at the drawings and identify the pairs of opposites.

> *AK* *There are four pairs of opposites:* up *and* down, into *and* out of, *away from* and *toward,* over *and* under.

Language Note: The preposition *above* is slightly different from *over. Above* does not imply as much movement. For example, *The plane is flying over the city.* BUT *The balloon is floating above the river.* (The balloon is moving a little but is more or less staying in the same place.)

b • Have students find the Kuroshio Current on the diagram and follow its path. Note that this activity begins with the Kuroshio Current and then follows the movement of other currents as they move around the Pacific Ocean.

Pronunciation: Kuroshio /kuroˈʃio/

> **In the Know:** When referring to the movement of water, a *drift* is similar to a *current*. In both cases, the water continually moves in a particular direction or pattern.

• Have students read the description and choose the correct prepositions by looking at the diagram.

> **AK** 1 *away from*   2 *across*   3 *toward*   4 *down*
> 5 *past*   6 *toward*   7 *past*   8 *around*

c • Before putting students in pairs, demonstrate this activity by describing a current and asking students which current it is.

• Put students in pairs to take turns describing different currents on the diagram in the same way.

• Follow up by asking random students to describe a current for the class to guess.

> **Optional Activity:** Have students describe something like the route of a train or bus using prepositions of movement. For example, *The train goes across the bridge, and then it goes into the tunnel at 96th Street.* Other ideas might include a pinball game or the operation of some kind of machine.

7 ▷ Language in Action: Directions

a • Tell students to cover the conversation and describe the situation in the picture. Ask *What are the people doing? (They're hiking.) Why do you think the couple is talking to the other man? (They're asking for directions.)*

• **AUDIO** Tell them to listen and answer the question *Is it possible to get to the trail they want?* Explain that a *trail* is a path, usually marked in some way for hikers to follow. Play the recording straight through.

• Have students read the conversation and their answers to the question.

> **AK** *Yes, they can get to the trail.*

b • Tell students to look at the conversation and the expressions in the box and try to fill in the blanks with the expressions. Check that students understand the expressions, especially *keep going = continue.*

• **AUDIO** Play the recording again for students to check their answers.

AK 2 *missed the turn*   3 *back that way*
4 *turn around and go back*   5 *keep going*
6 *stay on*   7 *follow*
8 *Go toward*

c • Put students in pairs to ask for and give directions to different places on the map.

• Follow up by asking one or two pairs to repeat one of their conversations for the class.

8 Listening

a • Have students look at this list of animals and say which they think are the most intelligent animals and which are the least intelligent. This could be done as a whole class or in small groups.

b • **AUDIO** Tell students to listen to the interview with Dr. Raul Calvi, who studies animal intelligence, and check the animals on the list that are mentioned. Play the recording straight through.

• Follow up by asking random students which animals were mentioned. Ask if any of the students can remember the context that the animals were mentioned in.

AK *Chimpanzees (learning language), gray parrot (naming 40 objects), and dogs and cats (rescuing people).*

c • Read through the statements and allow students to make guesses, but don't confirm or deny any suggestions.

• **AUDIO** Ask students to listen again to check their ideas and answer the ones they didn't remember.

• Follow up by asking random students for their answers and the reasons for choosing them.

• **AUDIO** If there is any doubt or disagreement, play the recording again, pausing at appropriate points for students to check.

AK 1 *T*   2 *F*   3 *F*   4 *F*   5 *T*   6 *T*

d • Work as a class to answer the questions.

9 Writing

a • Tell students they are going to write a paragraph about a special characteristic of an animal.

- Look at the example paragraph. This paragraph is about a specific animal, but tell students they can write about a type of animal in general if they prefer.

- Ask students to think about what they are going to write. Suggest that they make notes before they start.

- Give them time to write their paragraphs. Circulate and help when asked.

b • Put students in small groups to read each other's paragraphs and ask any questions they might have.

- **Option:** Post the paragraphs around the room and have students circulate to read the paragraphs.

- Follow up by asking students to discuss the most interesting or unusual paragraphs.

10 ▸ In Conversation

- Ask students to cover the conversation and describe the picture. Tell them that the people in the picture are Erica and Kenny.

- **AUDIO** Tell students to listen to the conversation and answer the questions *What is Kenny going to do? Is Erica going to join him?* Play the recording straight through.

- Check with the students, but don't accept or reject any answers.

- **AUDIO** Ask students to read the conversation to check their answers. Play the recording again while they are reading.

> **AK** *He's going to volunteer at the zoo.*
> *Yes, Erica may join him.*

11 ▸ Focus on Grammar

a • Have students look at the chart, fill in the blank, and answer the question.

> **AK** 1 *to*
> 2 With want *the negative is formed with the auxiliary* did + not.
> *For example, She didn't want them to…*
> (With asked *and* told *the word* not *is used before the infinitive. For example, …*not to arrive late.)

- Have students find four examples of reported requests in the conversation.

> **AK** *She asked me to come to a volunteer training session.*
> *And she told me to think about which animals I'd like to work with.*
> *She told me not to worry about that.*
> *Well, she wanted me to attend a session on Saturday, but I can't.*

b • Read through the prompts and go over the example sentence.

- **AUDIO** Tell students to listen to the volunteer training session. Play the recording straight through.

- **AUDIO** Tell students to listen again and report the instructions (1–6), using the prompts in the order they hear them.

c • Have students compare their answers with a partner.

- **AUDIO** Play the recording again for them to check the order.

- Follow up by asking random students for their answers.

> **AK** *2 She told them to take a name tag.*
> *3 She asked Kenny to begin.*
> *4 She told them to take a ten-minute break.*
> *5 She didn't want them to touch the animals.*
> *6 She told them not to feed the animals.*

d • Put students in pairs to take turns making requests. Tell them to remember what they were asked to do.

- Combine pairs into groups of four. Have students report their requests to the other pair.

> **Language Note:** *Ask* vs. *tell: Ask* is usually used to make a request and is often accompanied by the word *please*. It is more polite and less authoritarian than *tell*. *Tell* is most often used to report a command. Sometimes if people want to be very clear that something is an order, they will say, "I'm not asking you; I'm telling you!"

> **Optional Activity:** Write a list of requests and commands on a piece of paper, include some negatives. Read out the requests and have students do them. Then put students in pairs to try and report the requests and commands in the correct order.

12 ▸ *KnowHow*: Choosing vocabulary to learn

a • Have students look through the vocabulary in this unit and make lists according to what might be useful to the four people mentioned. This could be done individually and then compared with a partner.

• Follow up by asking random students for some of their words and the reasons they chose them.

   AK *Answers will vary.*

b • Tell students to choose five words from this unit that are useful for them.

• Put students in pairs or small groups to compare their words and explain why they chose them.

• **Option:** You could also ask students to explain what they are going to do to learn them.

13 ▸ Speaking

a • Remind students about the strategies to help with fluency in Unit 9. If necessary, have them look back at the suggestions.

• Put students in pairs to read the situations and choose an animal from the list for each one. They should also discuss the advantages and disadvantages of each animal for each situation.

• Tell students to write down the animals they chose and make notes about the advantages and disadvantages.

b • Split up the pairs and put students in small groups to compare and explain their choices.

• You could demonstrate the activity with one student or write a model sentence on the board. For example, *A good pet for (name) might be (pet name) because (reason).*

• **Option:** Have students mingle and talk to as many people as they can.

• Follow up by asking students how similar or different their choices were.

   AK *Answers will vary.*

12 The right approach

Main aims of this unit

Grammar:	Second conditional; making indirect questions
Vocabulary:	Expressions with *get, make,* and *take*; jobs and work
Functions:	Being polite

Unit Overview

Reading:	Extract: Dear Jean: What They Don't Teach You at the Water Cooler
Vocabulary:	Expressions with *get, make,* and *take*
Focus on Grammar:	Second conditional
Listening:	A radio call-in show
Vocabulary:	Jobs and work
Writing:	Asking for and giving advice
Speaking:	"The *If...* Game"
Reading:	Social Customs and Cultural Misunderstandings
In Conversation:	"Do you know what time I should arrive?"
Focus on Grammar:	Making indirect questions
KnowHow:	Intonation patterns
Language in Action:	Politeness

Warm-up

Give students an example of something that annoys you. For example, *I get mad when someone plays loud music late at night, but what can I do? I hate it when someone disturbs me when I'm preparing lessons, but what can I do?* Then ask students for examples of what annoys them, especially while working.

1 ▷ Reading

a • Tell students they are going to read an excerpt from a book of advice for people in the workplace. Read the title of the book. Ask students what they think it means.

> **In the Know:** Many offices have water coolers where people can get cold drinking water. It is natural for people to meet and have casual conversations "around the water cooler."

• Have students look at the picture and speculate about the problem shown. Ask *What kinds of topics do you think might be discussed?* Brainstorm possible problems on the board.

b • Have students cover the advice. Tell students to skim the problems quickly and think about what advice Jean will give.

• Follow up by asking students what the three problems are about and what they think Jean will say. Accept any suggestions.

c • Tell students to skim the advice quickly and check their predictions.

• Follow up by asking random students how similar or different their predictions were.

d • Have students read through the possible responses (a-b) for each of the three situations.

• Tell students to read the advice on page 95 again and decide which responses agree with Jean's advice.

• Students could compare their answers with a partner before the follow-up.

• Follow up by asking random students for the responses they chose and why.

> **AK** Situation 1: *b (Jean suggests bringing a radio with headphones OR taking turns to choose the radio station.)*
> Situation 2: *a (She says she would do nothing.)*
> Situation 3: *a (She suggests an indirect approach, asking the person if she's looking for something.)*

e • Have students read the relevant paragraphs again to find a word or expression for each definition.

• Follow up by asking random students for their answers.

> **AK** 1 *intrusive*   2 *make a scene*
> 3 *compromise*   4 *accessible*
> 5 *considerate*   6 *take the initiative*

f • Either have a class discussion or put students in small groups to discuss the questions.

• If students worked in small groups, follow up by asking each group to summarize their answers.

2 ▷ Vocabulary: Expressions with *get*, *make*, and *take*

a • Have students look at the diagrams and then look back at the texts and find more expressions for each verb.

• **Option:** Ask students to record this in their notebooks in the form of spidergrams with each verb in the middle. They could add more expressions they already know and also leave some "legs" of the spidergram empty so that they can add more later.

> **AK** get: *earplugs / permission*
> make: *a scene / life easier*
> take: *turns / the initiative / a look*

b • Ask students to choose one or two expressions from each diagram and write their own example sentence for each one.

• Put students in pairs to compare their sentences.

• ***Help Desk:*** Read through with the students. They could add these expressions to their spidergrams and write their own example sentences.

3 ▶ Focus on Grammar

a • Tell students to read the questions. Ask *Do these questions refer to a real situation or a hypothetical or imaginary situation?*

> **AK** *Hypothetical or imaginary situations.*

> **Language Note:** Second conditionals are used to express present unreal conditions. This means that the condition proposed in the *if* clause is not true. Therefore, the result or consequence in the main clause is also imaginary. For example, *If I had more time (but I don't), I would get my work done (but I won't!).*
>
> It is often difficult for students to grasp that these sentences refer to present situations but use past tense verbs.

b • Have students look at the chart and answer the questions.

> **AK** 1 *simple past*   2 would + *base form*

 • Draw students' attention to the note about the use of *were* in formal situations and especially in the expression *If I were you,…*

> **Language Note:** *If* clauses can appear either at the beginning of a sentence or at the end. When the *if* clause appears at the beginning of a sentence, place a comma at the end of the clause. For example, *If I were you, I would be happy.* When the *if* clause appears at the end of a sentence, no comma is needed. For example, *I would be happy if I were you.*

c • Tell students to look at the example. Then have them fill in the blanks using the verbs in parentheses to make second conditional sentences. Remind them to use contractions where possible.

 • Follow up by asking random students for their answers. For this exercise, make sure that students use *were*, not *was*, for the third person singular past of *be*.

> **Language Note:** The use of *were* for all persons in these sentences is still usual in American English. However, in informal speech it also very common for people to use *was*. This use of *were* is a leftover from an Old English subjunctive mood. Modern English has no subjunctive as a separate verb form, as some languages do.

AK 2 He'd get...were...
4 We'd get...didn't take...
6 ...wouldn't like...were...

3 ...would you do...didn't like...
5 ...made...she'd be...
7 ...started...they'd finish...

- **Option:** You could practice saying these sentences, concentrating on the contractions (*I'd, he'd, you'd, she'd, etc.*) and especially the question *What would you do if...?*

d • Have students make their own second conditional sentences, using the prompts or their own ideas. Ask them to write the sentences in their notebooks.

- Put students in pairs to compare sentences before the follow-up.

- Follow up by asking random students for one of their sentences, or ask all students for their sentences using one of the prompts to see how many different ideas they had.

> **Optional Activity:** Ask each student to write one *What would you do if...?* question on a sheet of paper and post them around the room. The questions could be serious or light-hearted. Have students circulate and write their answers under the questions. Then read out some of the most interesting answers.

4 Listening

a • Have students look at the picture and explain that they are going to listen to part of a radio program where people phone in to ask for advice on problems. The announcers giving advice are Alicia and Ryan.

- **AUDIO** Tell students to listen and say what the problems are. Play the recording straight through.

- **AUDIO** Follow up by asking students for their answers. If students are unable to give complete responses, encourage individuals to report any ideas they heard. Note these on the board. Play the recording a second time if necessary.

AK Problem 1: *personal e-mail at work*
Problem 2: *gossip at work*
Problem 3: *the owner's son is terrible at his job*

b • **AUDIO** Tell students to listen again and make notes on the advice given. Remind them to write only key words, not complete sentences.

- **AUDIO** If necessary, play the recording again, pausing at the end of each section.

151

- Give students time to review their notes on the advice and then have them compare their notes with a partner.

- Follow up by asking random students for their responses. Accept any reasonable responses. The answers below present some of the key ideas for each problem, but students' wording may vary.

> AK   Problem 1: *They told him to ask the friend to stop sending him e-mail at work. They also said he should take the initiative and talk to his boss.*
> Problem 2: *They told her to stay out of it as much as possible. They also said she should keep quiet or even leave the room. They also said she could tell people how she felt, but this might be "too direct."*
> Problem 3: *They told him there was nothing he could do. He might have to start looking for another job.*

c • Either have a class discussion or put students in small groups to express their opinions.

  • If students worked in groups, follow up by asking each group to summarize their discussion.

5 ▸ Vocabulary: Jobs and work

a • Tell students to read the sentences and put the underlined words in the correct diagrams based on the context.

  • Ask a few questions to check understanding. For example, *What's the difference between being fired and resigning? (Fired: being asked to leave one's job. Resigning: leaving a job because you want to.) What's the opposite of being fired? (Being hired.) Is being promoted a good or bad thing? (A good thing.)*

  • **Option:** Ask students to copy the spidergrams into their notebooks, leaving some "legs" empty for any more words they might want to add later.

AK

People	Hours & pay	Getting & keeping a job	Leaving a job
boss	work nine to five	hired	fired
	overtime	has (have) experience	resigned
	raise	be promoted	

Language Note: The examples present *hire* and *fire* in the passive form. For example, *She was hired because she has a lot of experience.* These words can also, of course, be used in the active sense. For example, *The company hired Janine because she had a lot of experience.*

In the Know: *Benefits* are extra payment or services given to employees in addition to their salary. For example, health insurance, paid vacation, etc.

b • Have students complete the paragraph with the correct form of the words from section 5a.

• Follow up by asking random students for their responses or by copying the paragraph onto the board and having students dictate the answers to a "secretary."

> **AK**   2 *employees*   3 *interview*   4 *hired*
> 5 *part-time*   6 *full-time* OR *nine to five*
> 7 *overtime*   8 *salary*   9 *raise*

Optional Activity: Play a game called *What's my job?* One student thinks of a job. The other students ask *yes / no* questions to discover what the job is. Count the *No* answers. If students don't guess the job before they have 10 (or any other number you choose) *No* answers, the student who thought of the job wins. You could also play this in small groups.

6 ▶ Writing

a • Look at the example. Have students write a note to another student asking for advice. Tell them the problem can be real or imaginary.

• Suggest some areas for students to think about, such as work or school, to keep the "problems" presented on a more impersonal or professional level.

b • **Option 1:** Have students exchange notes with a partner. Then they should write some advice for their partner's problem and give the note back.

• Then put students in small groups to read the problems and to discuss the advice. If students don't agree with the advice written on the note, they should give their own advice.

• Circulate and listen.

- **Option 2:** Ask students to take a full sheet of paper and fold the top over. Have students write their problem on the folded-over section and pass the paper to the next student.

- Tell students to write their advice on the paper below the problem and fold the top down further so that this piece of advice can't be seen. They then pass the paper to another student.

- Repeat this until there are four or five pieces of advice on the paper. Make sure students only read the problem, not other students' advice.

- Return the paper to the student who wrote the problem. This person reads all the advice and decides which is the best (or the funniest!).

- For either activity, follow up by asking how much of the advice students agreed on.

7 ▶ Speaking

a • Students need one die for each group and a marker for each player. The markers could be colored counters, buttons, or small pieces of paper labeled with the player's name.

- You could use coins instead of dice. Tell students to flip the coin and move forward two spaces if it lands heads up and three spaces if it lands on tails.

- Put students in small groups and ask them to use only one book in each group.

- Set a time limit of about 10 minutes since the game does not have a winner.

- Tell students to throw the die and answer the question they land on. Make sure they explain their answers.

- Circulate and listen. Follow up by asking each group for the most interesting answer from their group.

8 ▶ Reading

a • Tell students to imagine they are writing to a visitor to their country.

- Look at the example and ask students to individually write three pieces of advice. Then put students in small groups to compare their lists.

- Follow up by asking how much they agreed or disagreed on.

b • Look at the pictures. Make sure students understand that a *coaster* is used to protect a table or other surface when putting a glass or cup on it. Explain that the word *trash* is similar to garbage.

• Tell students to read the article quickly. Then have them decide which story each item relates to and explain how it's related.

• Follow up by asking random students for their answers and the reasons for them.

> **AK** Story 1: *A trash can and a mailbox. (The writer put the trash in the mailbox.)*
> Story 2: *A bouquet of flowers. (The writer gave the wrong number of flowers.)*
> Story 3: *A coaster. (The writer ate the coaster by mistake.)*

• You could ask a few additional questions to check understanding of the stories. *Story 1: Does the writer live in the United States? Who was he staying with and what were they doing? Story 2: Where was the writer? What is the custom in her country about giving flowers? Was the colleague angry? Story 3: Where did this take place? What did the Japanese hosts do when they saw the writer eating the coaster? Why?*

c • Have students read the article again. Either have a class discussion or put students in small groups to discuss the questions.

• To get the conversation going, first ask for one or two ideas in the whole class.

• If students worked in groups, follow up by asking each group to summarize their discussions for the class. Ask for any other particularly interesting comments.

9 ▶ In Conversation

• Ask students to cover the conversation and look at the picture.

• **AUDIO** Tell students they are going to listen to the conversation and that they should listen for three things the man asks about. Play the recording straight through.

• Check answers with the students, but don't accept or reject any suggestions.

• **AUDIO** Tell students to read the conversation and check their answers. Play the recording again while they are reading.

AK   *He asks…*
    1 *what he should take as a gift.*
    2 *what time he should arrive.*
    3 *where he can buy chocolates (near here).*

10 ▸ Focus on Grammar

a • Have students look at the chart comparing direct and indirect questions and then have them answer the questions.

• Demonstrate the point that indirect questions are more polite by asking volunteer students the same question in two ways. For example, *Where is the post office?* vs. *Excuse me, could you please tell me where the post office is?* Let your intonation show that the first question sounds rather abrupt and almost rude.

AK   1 *In indirect questions, the subject comes before the verb, as in statement order.*
    2 Yes / no *questions.*
    3 *No.*

> **Language Note:** If students ask why the question is in statement form, explain that the question is in the beginning. For example, *Do you know…? Can you tell me…?*

b • Tell students to write the questions in their notebooks, using different beginnings. Follow up by asking random students for their answers.

AK   *Beginnings of the indirect questions will vary.*
    1 *…where the conference room is?*
    2 *…when the post office closes?*
    3 *…where your colleagues went?*
    4 *…if there is a nice restaurant near here?*
    5 *…why Maya left work early?*
    6 *…what time the party starts?*

c • Put students in pairs to make conversations with indirect questions. Circulate and listen.

• Follow up by asking random pairs to repeat one of their conversations for the class.

11 ▶ *KnowHow*: Intonation patterns

> **Language Note:** Explain that *intonation* is the rise and fall of your voice while you are speaking.

a • **AUDIO** Tell students to listen to the two conversations and say which one has a greater range of intonation and sounds more polite. Play the recording straight through.

  • Ask students why the conversation they chose sounded more polite.

  > **AK** *The second recording of the conversation sounds more polite. It also has the greater range of intonation.*

  • Have students practice the conversation that has the greater range of intonation.

b • **AUDIO** Play the recording of the conversation and have students repeat.

  • Either show the stress and intonation with your hands or write the sentences on the board with the intonation shown as a line.

  • You can exaggerate the intonation at first, since most students will use less intonation than the model.

  • Put students in pairs to practice the intonation.

> **Optional Activity:** English has a measurably greater range of intonation than some other languages. To experiment with this in the classroom, play a recording of people speaking English. You could play something from one of the previous units, which students have already heard. As students listen, have them do something to indicate the intonation patterns they hear. For example, they could move their hands up and down, as if conducting an orchestra! OR They could clap their hands or tap out the rhythm with a pencil. Then using the audioscripts in the back of the book, have students practice reading the script, focusing on the intonation.

12 ▶ Language in Action: Politeness

a • Look at the pictures and have students describe what they think is happening in each one.

  • **AUDIO** Tell them to listen to the conversations and match them to the pictures. Play the recording straight through.

  • Follow up by asking random students for their answers.

  > **AK** A 2   B 3   C 1

b • Look at the expressions and ask students to write the number of the conversation they think each one comes in.

  • **Audio** Tell students to listen again and check. Play the recording again straight through.

  • Follow up by asking random students for their answers.

AK

Being Polite	
1 Let me give you my card.	3 We'd like you to have this.
1 Here's my card.	3 How nice!
1 Please contact me any time.	3 It's my pleasure.
1, 2, 3 Thank you.	1 I'll be in touch.
2 Would you be able to…?	1 It was nice to meet you.
2 I'd really appreciate it if…	1 Have a good trip (back).
2 I'll see what I can do.	1 Goodbye.

c • Put students in pairs to make their own conversations using the expressions.

  • Remind them to use a good range of intonation.

Units 10–12 Review

Grammar

1 *Possible answer:*
You should avoid being the tallest object in an area, and you should stay away from trees. You should get to a building, too.

2 2 *will be / go*   3 *will be / are*

3 2 *ought OR are supposed to*
3 *Should*
4 *ought OR are supposed*
5 *should not (shouldn't)*
6 *are not (aren't) supposed*
7 *better*

4 2 *...them to attend the meeting for me.*
3 *...me to greet the visitor.*
4 *...me to call (her) right away.*

5 1 *had*   2 *would make*   3 *took*   4 *would make*

6 2 *...if everybody knows about the meeting?*
3 *...who the main speaker is?*
4 *...what they are going to discuss?*
5 *...what they talked about (at the last meeting)?*

Vocabulary

7 1 *take over*   2 *make*   3 *coast*   4 *get*
5 *take on*   6 *raise*   7 *pull over*

8 1 *wear*   2 *bring*   3 *missed*
4 *meet*   5 *watching*

Recycling Center

9 2 *doing / making*   3 *do / do / made*
4 *make / make*   5 *doing / made*

Fun Spot

Resign = to leave your job or position
Employee = a person who works for somebody
Coast = the area of land that is next to or close to the ocean
River = a large, natural stream of water
Host = a person who receives a guest

Phonetic Symbols

VOWELS

i	be	/bi/
ɪ	British	/ˈbrɪtɪʃ/
ɛ	yes	/yɛs/
æ	ask	/æsk/
ɑ	not	/nɑt/
ɔ	call	/kɔl/
ʊ	foot	/fʊt/
u	do	/du/
ʌ	lunch	/lʌntʃ/
ə	Canada	/ˈkænədə/
eɪ	name	/neɪm/
aɪ	nice	/naɪs/
ɔɪ	voice	/vɔɪs/
aʊ	house	/haʊs/
oʊ	note	/noʊt/
ər	work	/wərk/
ɪr	here	/hɪr/
ɛr	pair	/pɛr/
ɑr	park	/pɑrk/
ɔr	Norway	/ˈnɔrweɪ/
ʊr	tourist	/ˈtʊrɪst/

CONSONANTS

p	please	/pliz/
b	boy	/bɔɪ/
t	teacher	/ˈtitʃər/
t̬	party	/ˈpɑrt̬i/
d	dinner	/ˈdɪnər/
k	class	/klæs/
g	good	/gʊd/
tʃ	chart	/tʃɑrt/
dʒ	Japan	/dʒəˈpæn/
f	phone	/foʊn/
v	verb	/vərb/
θ	think	/θɪŋk/
ð	this	/ðɪs/
s	say	/seɪ/
z	Brazil	/brəˈzɪl/
ʃ	show	/ʃoʊ/
ʒ	television	/ˈtɛləvɪʒn/
h	he	/hi/
m	meet	/mit/
n	nine	/naɪn/
ŋ	beginning	/bɪˈgɪnɪŋ/
l	level	/ˈlɛvl/
r	read	/rid/
y	you	/yu/
w	word	/wərd/

Keep on talking!

General presentation tips

- These activities can be used towards the end of the unit or as a follow-up activity.

- The time limits are only suggestions, and you should judge when to give more time or to move on before the suggested time.

- When the activity has Part A and Part B, put students in pairs, A and B. Get them to sit facing each other. Then tell all the A's to look at page X and all the B's to look at Page Y. They should not look at their partner's information.

- When the activity involves a discussion or group decision, have students brainstorm useful phrases onto the board before starting the discussion.

- When students are working, circulate and listen, but don't interfere unless there are really serious problems. Note any common mistakes to practice in a later class. Help with vocabulary when asked.

Unit 1 ▸ Personal bingo

- Read through the instructions with the students so that they understand the activity.
- Put students in pairs to fill in the empty squares on their bingo cards.
- Set a time limit of about five minutes for this.
- Circulate and help with ideas if necessary. For example, *doesn't mind cooking / hopes to learn another language / would like to work with animals / wants to change his/her job / went to the gym yesterday / plays a musical instrument / relaxed with friends last night, etc.*
- If you feel it is necessary, practice the questions for the set items on the cards before they start the next part of the activity. *Did you have a good time last weekend? Did you wash the dishes last night? Do you often unwind by walking in the park? Do you like to iron? Would you like to go scuba diving? Did you have a hard day yesterday?*
- When students are ready, have them circulate and ask questions about the items on their card.
- If the first student to complete a line does so very quickly, you could allow the students to continue for a few more minutes to find out who comes "second."

Unit 2 ▸ What do you know about language?

- Put students in pairs to try to answer the questions.
- Tell them to discuss the questions and guess which answer they think is most likely correct. They are not expected to know all the answers.

> **Pronunciation:** linguists /ˈlɪŋgwɪsts/   Basque /bæsk/
> tycoon /taɪˈkuːn/   consonant /ˈkɑnsənənt/
> gobbledygook /ˈgɑbəldiˌgʊk/   buckaroo /ˌbəkəˈruː/

- Set a time limit of about five minutes.
- When students have answered (or guessed) all the questions, join pairs to compare and discuss their answers.
- Tell them to look at page 111 to check.

   AK 1 *b*   2 *a*   3 *c*   4 *c*   5 *d*   6 *b*   7 *d*

> **In the Know:** Basque, spoken by about 500,000 people in the north of Spain and neighboring parts of France, does not relate to any other European language.
>
> All radio communications between pilots and air traffic control are in English.
>
> *Tycoon* comes from the Japanese word *taikun*, an old word for shogun, a military commander.
>
> *Gobbledygook* is a twentieth century word, probably formed from *gobble* (the sound made by turkeys).
>
> *Buckaroo* comes from the Spanish *vaquero* (cowboy).

Unit 3 ▶ Been there, done that

- Read through the instructions with the students so that they understand the activity.

- Put students in pairs to fill in the chart with the names of three specific items for each category.

- Set a time limit of about three minutes for this.

- Have students circulate and ask questions to find people who have done these things. Tell students to take notes of what other students have or haven't done.

- Set a time limit of about five to seven minutes for this.

- Bring the class together to compare notes.

- Ask pairs to say which of their items most people have done, seen, played, etc.

- Ask if there were any items nobody has done, seen, played, etc.

Unit 4 ▶ Locked out!

- This is an information exchange activity.

- Put students in pairs facing each other. Decide who is A and who is B.

- Have the A's look at page 106 and the B's look at page 109. They should read their sentences to each other and put the story in logical order, without looking at their partner's page. Tell students to look at the picture for help.

> **Pronunciation:** Sheila /ˈʃilə/   Doug /dʌg/

- Set a time limit of about six to eight minutes for this activity.

- Have students tell their versions of the story. Ask *What's the next sentence?* If there is disagreement, ask students to explain the reasons for their choices.

> **AK** *Sheila had the scariest experience of her life last year.*
> *One warm but windy morning, Sheila was reading a book in the living room of her apartment on the third floor of a small apartment building.*
> *Suddenly, the wind blew her bedroom door shut.*
> *Sheila tried to open the door, but it was locked and she didn't have the key.*
> *She asked her next door neighbor Doug to help her, so Doug went to find a locksmith.*
> *But when Doug came back, he was holding a long rope in his hand.*
> *He said, "All of the locksmiths are closed, but I have an idea! We'll use this rope."*
> *Ten minutes later, Sheila was standing in the window of Doug's living room.*
> *Doug was standing on the roof of the building, holding one end of the rope.*
> *The other end of the rope was tied around Sheila's body, just under her arms.*
> *Doug counted to three.*
> *On three, Sheila swung from his living room window to her bedroom window, which was only about ten feet away.*
> *While she was swinging in the air, Doug said, "Don't look down!"*
> *She didn't, and believe it or not, she made it safely into her bedroom.*

Unit 5 ▸ The world of advertising

- Read through the instructions to make sure the students understand the activity.

- Put students in small groups.

- Set a time limit of about five minutes for the groups to discuss the photograph and the questions.

- In groups, have students think of a product they would like to advertise. Set a time limit of about ten minutes for the groups to discuss the questions and create their advertisement.

- Make sure the groups decide how they are going to present their advertisement to the class: one individual doing the presentation or the group sharing the presentation.

- When they are ready, have each group present their advertisement to the class.

- Remind the other students to ask questions to try to guess what the product being advertised is.

Unit 6 ▸ What's important!

- Read through the instructions with the students.

- If necessary, review the vocabulary in the chart.

> **Pronunciation:** honest /'anɪst/   eccentric /ɪk'sentrɪk/
> ambitious /æm'bɪʃəs/   stubborn /'stʌbərn/

- Put students in pairs to choose the three most important personality characteristics for each profession.

- There should be an even number of pairs. If this is not possible, make some groups of three.

- Set a time limit of about six to eight minutes for this.

- Put pairs together to make groups of four to compare their charts and explain the reasons for their answers.

- Follow up by asking each group for the characteristics they agreed on.

Unit 7 ▸ Entrepreneurs /ˌantrəprə'nʊrz/

- As this activity involves several groups of "Entrepreneurs" presenting ideas to one group of "Investors," you may need to divide a large class. In this case, make three groups of "Entrepreneurs" for every group of "Investors."

- Put students in small groups and decide which groups are "Entrepreneurs" and which groups are the "Investors."

- Make sure each group understands what they should do. Set a time limit of about eight minutes, but be prepared to give more time if the groups get very involved.

- Have the "Investors" sit apart from the other groups while they list the kind of businesses they think would be successful so that the groups cannot overhear their discussion. If they finish before the others are ready, ask them to list the businesses in order of importance to the community.

- Make sure the "Entrepreneurs" decide how they are going to present their ideas to the "Investors."

- When the "Entrepreneurs" are ready, have them present their ideas to the "Investors."

- Follow up by asking the "Investors" to say which ideas they think would be most successful. Ask them to explain why.

Unit 8 ▸ A communication crossword

- Before starting this activity, give students examples of clues for different words. For example, *It's something you do every day. You do it with water, coffee, tea, etc.* (DRINK) *It's the past tense of* go. (WENT) *This person works in a school. She gives classes.* (TEACHER)

- Then have students practice producing clues for other words. DOG, MONTH, DRIVER, UNDER, *etc.*

- Put students in pairs facing each other. Decide who is A and who is B. Make sure they don't let their partner see their crossword puzzle.

- Have the A's look at page 108 and the B's look at page 111.

- Check that students understand *across* and *down* in the crossword.

- Set a time limit of about eight minutes. Circulate and help if any students are having problems making up clues.

- When students have finished, have them compare their crosswords.

Unit 9 ▸ Thirty years ago

- Give students a few minutes to think individually about how their community has changed in the last 20 to 30 years and make their lists.

- Tell them to look at the picture to help with ideas.

- Put students in pairs to discuss their lists and decide which changes are positive and which are negative.

- Follow up by having one pair report their opinions to the class. Ask for similar or differing opinions as each point is mentioned.

- Ask a second pair to report any different changes they have listed, so that there is no repetition.

- Then do the same with the other pairs.
- If the class is large, the follow-up could be done in two or three large groups.

Unit 10 ▸ Tried and true?

- Put the students into pairs. Decide which are Pair A's and which are Pair B's.
- There should be an even number of pairs. If this is not possible, make some groups of three.
- Pair A's should look at page 110 and Pair B's at page 111.
- Read through the instructions for Part 1.
- Set a time limit of about five minutes for the pairs to discuss their expressions and decide on their presentations.

> **Pronunciation:** broth /brɔθ/   hatched /hætʃt/

- Circulate and listen. Help if students are stuck for an explanation of an expression.
- Join Pairs A and B so that each pair can present their expressions to the other pair.
- Encourage students to make comments during the presentations.
- When students have finished, you could ask if there are similar expressions in their languages.

> **In the Know:** *Don't judge a book by its cover*: Don't form opinions based only on appearances.
>
> *Look before you leap*: Think before you act.
>
> *Too many cooks spoil the *broth*: Too many people working on the same thing don't produce good results. **a type of soup*
>
> *Don't put all your eggs in one basket*: Don't concentrate all your efforts on one project.
>
> *Don't count your chickens before they are hatched*: Don't start planning on the results of a project before it is finished.
>
> *Many hands make light work*: Many people working together make the work easy.

Unit 11 Where could this be?

- Put students in pairs facing each other. Decide who is A and who is B.

- Have the A's look at page 110 and the B's look at page 112. Read through the instructions.

- Write these extra questions on the board. For the A's: *What's in the background of the picture? Do people live and work here? What might they do?* For the B's: *What's the weather like here? Do people live and work here? What might they do?*

- Set a time limit of about six to eight minutes for discussions of both photographs.

- Then have the students tell each other about the pictures.

> **In the Know:** The Uyuni Salt Flats in Bolivia are the world's largest salt flats. They cover an area of 12,000 sq. miles and are at an altitude of 3,653 meters. They were a part of a prehistoric lake which covered most of Bolivia. When it dried up, it left a couple of small lakes and several salt pans. There is also a hotel there, made entirely of salt.
>
> The Giants' Causeway in Northern Ireland is a natural formation of volcanic rock, but, according to legend, it was built for giants to travel across to Scotland.

Unit 12 Role-play: I'm so sorry...

- Put students in pairs facing each other. Decide who is A and who is B.

- Have the A's look at Role Card A and the B's look at Role Card B.

- Set a time limit of about six to eight minutes for students to work together to create a role-play.

- Encourage students to continue the conversation beyond the basic apology and acceptance.

- Have students change partners and repeat the activity without rehearsal.

- Follow up by asking volunteers to perform their role-play for the class.

Workbook Answer Key

UNIT 1

1
2 makes
3 cost
4 finished
5 worked
6 didn't have
7 had
8 lost
9 asked
10 was
11 went
12 talked
13 laughed
14 returned
15 causes
16 helps
17 does not (doesn't) think
18 does not (doesn't) take
19 relaxes
20 makes

2
2 a hard day
3 to get together with
4 by myself
5 to get away
6 to relax
7 work hard
8 to do chores

3
2 a
3 c
4 b
5 b

4
2 did
3 has
4 does
5 are
6 have

5
2 Neither do
3 So did
4 Neither have

6
2 What about you?
3 Where do you live?
4 What's Chicago like?
5 It was nice to meet you.

7
2 Tony
3 Mike
4 Joanna and Carla
5 Laura
6 Pam
8 doesn't mind sweeping the floor
9 can't stand taking out the garbage
10 doesn't mind ironing the clothes
11 need to do the laundry
12 need to wash the car

8
2 socializing
3 cooking
4 doing
5 living
6 to clean
7 waking up
8 to call
9 to find

9 Answers will vary.

UNIT 2

1
a am ('m) buying
b is getting
c am ('m) typing
2 Nothing much. How are you?
3 I'm OK. I'm typing this on my new computer.

4 Finally! You had a very old one!
I'm buying a cell phone with
instant text messaging next
month.
5 You love technology, don't you?
6 I do. But I'll have to learn to
type on those small keys.
7 You'll learn fast. My sister has
one of those, and her typing is
getting faster these days.
8 It is? Maybe she'll give me
"typing lessons." OK, (I've) got
to go.
9 OK, see you soon!

2 2 am ('m) sitting
3 are ('re) staying
4 are ('re) looking
5 are ('re) visiting
6 am ('m) studying
7 am ('m) getting
8 am ('m) meeting
9 are ('re) going

3 1 We are (We're) going to a
soccer game this weekend.
2 It is (It's) getting hotter.
Fred's nephews are growing all
the time.

4 2 gets angry
3 get there
4 get some stamps
5 getting a cell phone
6 get better
7 got colder
8 got home

5 2 celebrate
3 educate
4 excitement
5 exploration
6 imagination
7 govern
8 management
9 translate
10 curiosity
11 creative
12 darkness

13 good
14 happiness
15 kindness
16 possibility
17 sadness
18 similar
19 sleepiness
20 stupidity

6 2 Education
3 possibility
4 government
5 celebration
6 imagination
7 achievement

7 1 what does "achievement" mean
2 is it a noun
3 How many syllables does it have

8 2 hear
3 hear
4 see
5 Look
6 see
7 listen

9 2 are / thinking
3 don't understand
4 am ('m) looking
5 are ('re) doing
6 love
7 hate
8 need
9 sounds
10 don't believe

UNIT 3

1 2 hear
3 feel
4 smell
5 taste

2 b 1
c 4
d 3
e 2
f 6

170

3 2 already
  3 still
  4 already
  5 yet
  6 yet

4 2 I haven't watched this video yet.
  3 The movie has already started.
  4 They still haven't shown the documentary on TV.
  5 I have already seen that movie.
  6 She still hasn't called the director.
  7 I haven't finished reading the script yet.

5 2 I don't think
  3 If you ask me
  4 I disagree
  5 But I still don't think
  6 Let's agree to disagree on this one

6 2 confusing
  3 bored
  4 exciting
  5 confused
  6 fascinating
  7 disappointed

7 1 frustrated
  2 tired
  3 relaxed
  4 relaxing
  5 surprised

8 2 didn't need to
  3 had to
  4 aren't allowed to
  5 had to
  6 didn't have to
  7 don't have to
  8 need to

9 Answers will vary.

10 Answers will vary.

UNIT 4

1 2 already
  3 still
  4 yet
  5 already
  6 still
  7 yet
  8 still

2 2 T
  3 F Gordon has already gotten a master's degree (in architecture).
  4 F Alicia has already gotten a job.
  5 T
  6 F Alicia hasn't written a book about her experiences yet. OR Alicia still hasn't written a book about her experiences.

3 2 were playing
  3 was studying
  4 knocked
  5 was trying
  6 was
  7 talked
  8 said
  9 was working
  10 remembered
  11 shouted

4 2 Someone knocked on the door while they were eating.
  3 Gordon was moving the furniture when his uncle called.
  4 I was reading a book when I heard the dog bark.
  5 The student asked a question while the teacher was talking.
  6 We were sitting in the park when it started to rain.

5 2 busier
  3 more polluted
  4 noisier
  5 less friendly
  6 smaller

7 quieter
8 more pleasant
9 less expensive
10 worse

6 2 more expensive than
3 as safe as
4 less friendly than
5 less noisy than
6 larger than
7 less famous than
8 as pleasant as

7 2 Tulsen U is not as expensive as Nelvor U.
3 Nelvor U is not as friendly as Tulsen U.
4 Tulsen U is not as noisy as Nelvor U.
5 Tulsen U is not as large as Nelvor U.
6 Tulsen U is not as famous as Nelvor U.

8 2 absent-minded
3 forget
4 remember
5 Remind

9 2 c
3 d
4 b
5 a
6 e
Answers will vary.

10 2 can't think
3 me think
4 the tip of my tongue
5 come to me
6 think of it in a minute

11 2 busier
3 more difficult
4 more relaxed
5 easier

UNIT 5

1 2 wanted
3 bought
4 was working OR worked
5 did not (didn't) have
6 asked
7 were walking OR walked
8 gave

2 1 more important than
2 cheaper than
3 less comfortable than
4 less romantic than

3 …It's the perfect gift for a music lover who likes to stay clean!

Do you live in a place with lots of insects that bother you? Do you have a child who can't sleep in the dark?…It's a very useful night-light that also kills insects!

Are you the kind of person who likes to read in bed, but doesn't like to sit up in bed? Try these bed glasses, with mirrors that reflect the light.…

4 2 b
3 d
4 a
5 f
6 e

2 Tony is a guitarist who plays in clubs.
3 There is a store near here that OR which sells nice clothes.
4 We live in a house that OR which has a swimming pool.
5 Martin has two children who love sports.
6 A chef is a person who cooks food in a restaurant.

5 2 Yes, she has produced many paintings <u>that</u> have sold all over the world.
3 She works in a little room <u>that</u> is at the top of the house.
4 And she uses a computer <u>that</u> is probably very expensive.
5 He is an artist <u>who</u> makes silver jewelry.
6 They looked like the kids <u>who</u> are in Susan's cartoons.

6 2 gold
3 leather
4 diamond
5 cotton
6 glass

7 2 it's small
3 it looks like
4 You use it to
5 Do you know the name of it
6 I'm not sure what it's called

8 2 microwave oven / cook or heat food
3 DVD player / playing DVDs
4 remote control / control the TV

9 1 Turn on
2 press the "play" button
3 turning up the volume
4 press the "eject" button

10 2 picks his glasses up OR picks up his glasses
3 puts them on
4 puts the keys down OR puts down the keys
5 turn the volume down OR turn down the volume
6 takes off his glasses OR takes his glasses off
7 puts them away
8 throw it away

UNIT 6

1 2 that
3 that
4 who
5 that
6 that
7 who

2 2 in
3 to
4 about
5 to
6 about
Answers to the second part of the exercise will vary.

3 Answers will vary.

4 1 similar to
2 good at OR interested in
3 interested in OR good at
4 surprised at

5 2 since
3 for
4 since
5 for

6 2 an hour and a half
3 an hour
4 a year

7 2 Meg and I have known each other for 9 years.
3 We moved to this house (about) five months ago.
4 Theresa bought a new car two days ago.
5 I haven't seen Tim since February (8, 1982).

8 2 It's nice to meet you
3 I think we've met before OR you look familiar
4 You look familiar OR I think we've met before
5 Do you know
6 That's why I recognize you

9 2 starting
3 listening
4 Going
5 Talking
6 Staying
7 learning
8 studying

10 Order of answers and the personal answers will vary.

11 2 unpopular
3 impatient
4 unenthusiastic
5 unkind
6 impolite
7 disagreeable

12 Answers will vary.

13 Answers will vary.

UNIT 7

1 1 Have we met before?
2 You look familiar.
3 That's why I recognize you!

2 2 has worked
3 did not (didn't) notice
4 went
5 did not (didn't) see

3 2 owed
3 bought
4 couldn't afford
5 lent
6 pay it back
7 spent
8 wasted
9 save
10 spend

4 1b lend
2a borrow
2b lend
2c lend

5 2 doesn't it
3 didn't you
4 were they
5 isn't it

6 2 did I
3 weren't we
4 didn't you
5 doesn't he
6 aren't they
7 was it
8 is she

7 A
2 **Brenda:** No way! You paid last time.
3 **Esther:** No, I didn't.
4 **Brenda:** Look, it's ten dollars for two cups of coffee. That's expensive.
5 **Esther:** No, it isn't. It's my treat.
6 **Brenda:** Oh, OK then. But I'll definitely pay next time!

B
2 **Alison:** Yes. Can I cash this check, please?
3 **Teller:** Sure. Can I see some identification, please?
4 **Alison:** Of course. Here's my passport.
5 **Teller:** Thanks. How would you like your cash?
6 **Alison:** Tens and twenties, please.

8 2 Could you do me a favor, please?
3 Gary doesn't make much money as an artist.
4 Have you done the laundry yet?
5 I'm making dinner tonight.
6 She's gone into town to do some shopping.
7 Leo finds it very hard to make decisions.
8 Can you make a living here?

9 A
2 will ('ll) probably do
3 are going to go
4 will ('ll) eat
5 will ('ll) come

B
2 am ('m) going to fix
3 will ('ll) help
4 am ('m) going to paint
5 will ('ll) help

10 Answers will vary.

UNIT 8

1 2 don't we
3 isn't it
4 don't we
5 don't you
6 didn't you

2 2 was recorded
3 is invited
4 is chosen
5 were presented
6 was replaced

3 2 T
3 F *Supercook* is watched by a lot of people.
4 T
5 F The first show was presented by Tom O'Donnell. OR
The first show wasn't presented by Matt Carter.

4 Answers will vary. Some possible answers:
Their car was made in Sydney.
That book was written by a famous person.
The computer was invented in 1946.
The store was painted yesterday.
Their car was painted yesterday.
The store was built by engineers.

5 2 Pasta was invented in China.
3 Our coffee isn't kept in the refrigerator.
4 This oven was built by my grandfather.
5 Portuguese was spoken at the meeting.
6 The research is paid for by the food association.

6 2 Peel
3 slice
4 Chop OR Cut
5 fry
6 Add

7 2 I have no idea
3 I didn't know that
4 That's the reason that
5 Did you know that

8 2 traffic
3 time
4 work
5 clothing
6 jewelry
7 luggage
8 pasta
9 fruit
10 meat
11 science
12 economics
13 Chinese
14 information

9 2 is
3 was
4 were
5 was
6 was
7 are
8 were
9 is
10 is

10 2 a little
3 a few
4 a few
5 a lot of
6 a few
7 a few

11 2 Correct
3 Our children are playing in <u>the</u> yard.
4 Can you pass <u>the</u> hot sauce, please?
5 Correct
6 Vegetarians don't eat (no article) meat.
7 (No article) French is a very interesting language.
8 Correct

UNIT 9

1 2 were not (weren't) treated
3 was given
4 were offered
5 were suggested
6 was not (wasn't) finished
7 were woken up
8 was taken
9 was joined
10 was left

2 2 the
3 the
4 the
5 the
6 the
7 the
8 the
9 N
10 N

3 2 visa
3 traveler's checks
4 check in
5 carry-on bag
6 window seat
7 aisle seat
8 made a reservation

9 reception desk
10 lobby
11 unpack your suitcase
12 sightseeing
13 pictures
14 map
15 get lost

4 2 has ('s) been working
3 has ('s) been traveling
4 have ('ve) been waiting
5 have not (haven't) been studying
6 have ('ve) been trying

5 2 What have you been doing there?
3 Have you been learning new things?
4 How many hours per week have you been working?
5 Have you been taking those classes?

6 2 He has (He's) been helping
3 He has (He's) been learning
4 He has (He's) been working
5 He has (He's) been taking

7 A
2 That's OK. I'll pay it.
3 There's a train tonight
4 That's great. Could you make the change, please?

B
1 I have a reservation.
2 Yes, Marvin Benson.
3 Certainly.
4 Thank you very much.

8 2 on the radio
3 in touch
4 by mistake
5 by chance
6 by hand
7 on purpose

9 3 She didn't use to work for a large company.
4 She didn't use to go out for dinner (with friends).
5 She used to wear jeans.
6 She used to take the bus (to the university).

10 2 Did you use to work
3 did you use to get
4 Did you use to drive
5 Did you use to go
6 did you use to wear

UNIT 10

1 2 did you use to believe
3 used to think
4 used to carry
5 used to happen
6 used to believe

2 2 met
3 look at
4 won
5 bring
6 carry
7 wear
8 use
9 loses

3 2 won't rain / is
3 sweeps / won't get
4 say / won't see
5 itches / will ('ll) get
6 don't throw / will ('ll) have

4 2 If your left hand itches, you will (you'll) lose some money.
3 If you eat cheese before going to bed, you will (you'll) have bad dreams.
4 If a black cat crosses your way, you will (you'll) have bad luck.
5 If you open an umbrella inside a building, it will bring bad luck.
6 If you sing before 7:00, you will (you'll) cry before 11:00.

5 A
2 come on
3 positive
4 believe it
5 be true

B
1 doubt
2 too much
3 works
4 expect

6 2 ought to
3 had better
4 should
5 shouldn't
6 aren't supposed to

7 2 He'd better not make too much noise.
3 They'd better not run.
4 She'd better turn off the stove.
5 You're supposed to look through the small end.
6 You're not supposed to park here.

8 2 got out
3 picked / up
4 got in
5 got off
6 give / back
7 sat down
8 stood up

9 Answers will vary.

UNIT 11

1 2 You ought to bring a camera.
3 You'd better bring warm clothing.
4 You're supposed to send your final payment 30 days before the start of the trip.
5 You should bring binoculars to look for birds.
6 You'd better not get too close to the waterfalls.

7 You're supposed to bring a backpack.
8 You're not supposed to wear sandals when hiking.

2 2 mountain
3 waterfall
4 river
5 mountains
6 island

3 2 could
3 must
4 might
5 can't

4 2 could OR may OR might OR must
3 can't
4 could OR may OR might OR must
5 must
6 can't
7 could
8 must

5 2 Yvonne's brother may OR might OR could be here on business.
3 Michelle could OR may OR might know the answers.
4 She must be Martha's daughter.
5 Could cats be highly intelligent?
6 These theories can't be true.
7 They can't be telling the truth.

6 2 toward
3 over OR across
4 across OR over
5 away from
6 around
7 into OR toward

7 2 ahead
3 going
4 turn
5 way
6 around
7 Stay
8 past

8 2 She told him not to leave the doors unlocked.
3 She asked him to feed the dog in the morning.
4 She told him not to feed the dog too much.
5 She wanted him to turn off the lights at night OR turn the lights off at night.
6 She asked him to cut the grass on Saturday.
7 She asked him not to pay the cleaners.
8 She wanted him to pick her up from the airport on Sunday.

9 Answers will vary.

UNIT 12

1 2 might
3 can't
4 can't

2 2 get
3 taking
4 get
5 making
6 take
7 made
8 made
9 take

3 2 e
3 d
4 h
5 a
6 g
7 b
8 f

4 3 wouldn't call
4 wanted
5 were
6 would ('d) talk
7 wouldn't be
8 were
9 wouldn't read

10 could
11 found out
12 would ('d) get
13 were
14 wouldn't try
15 would ('d) love
16 weren't

5 2 If Jonathan weren't late again, his boss wouldn't be angry. OR Jonathan's boss wouldn't be angry if Jonathan weren't late again.
3 If Lilian weren't ill, she would go to work today. OR Lilian would go to work today if she weren't ill.
4 If Rob knew how to use the computer, he would do the job. OR Rob would do the job if he knew how to use the computer.
5 If Paul and Jack weren't wearing shorts, they would be allowed into the restaurant. OR Paul and Jack would be allowed into the restaurant if they weren't wearing shorts.
6 If Ms. Thomson weren't in a meeting, she would see you now. OR Ms. Thomson would see you now if she weren't in a meeting.

6 2 Who would you call if you saw a burglar going into your neighbor's house?
3 What would you say to your boss if he or she offered you a better salary?
4 How would you react if you won a new car on a game show?
5 If you could live anywhere in the world, where would you choose?

Answers to the questions will vary.

7 2 salaries
3 overtime
4 part-time
5 employees
6 retire
7 be promoted
8 clients
9 interviews
10 apply

8 2 Could you tell me what time the interview starts?
3 Do you know where the restroom keys are?
4 Can you tell me how many hours a week you work?
5 Do you have any idea how old Steven was when he retired?
6 Does your boss know when your meeting is?

9 2 Could you tell me what number bus I should take?
3 Do you have any idea where the bus stop is?
4 Do you know how often the buses arrive?
5 Can you tell me how much a ticket costs?

10 2 Let me give you my card.
3 Please contact me any time.
4 It was nice to meet you.
5 Have a good trip back.

UNITS 1–3
READING

1 b 5   c 6
   d 2   e 1
   f 4

2 2 made *One Week*
   3 broke his neck
   4 signed with MGM
   5 made *The Cameraman*
   6 his friend Fatty Arbuckle died
   7 married for the third time

3 2 f   3 a
   4 e   5 d
   6 c

4 2 *The Cameraman.*
   3 *The General.*
   4 In 1923.
   5 *One Week* and *My Wife's Relations.*

UNITS 4–6
READING

1 b

2 1 1946
   2 1947
   3 1966

3 2 laboratory
   3 explode
   4 domestic
   5 uniform
   6 stir

4 1 F Dr. Spencer wasn't looking for a new way to cook food when he discovered the microwave.
OR
Dr. Spencer was testing a new piece of radar technology called "magnetron" when he discovered the microwave.
   2 T
   3 F Not everyone loved microwave cooking at first.

4 F You can't use all types of dishes in a microwave oven.
OR
You can only use microwave-safe dishes in a microwave oven.
5 T

UNITS 7–9
READING

1 b 1st
   c 2nd
   d 4th
   e 3rd

2 2 e   3 a
   4 b   5 c

3 1 b   2 a
   3 b   4 a
   5 c   6 a

UNITS 10–12
READING

1 a 3
   b 1, 3
   c 3, 4
   d 4

2 2 Kelly
   3 a small piece of paper
   4 tearing off a piece of paper (and trading it for a fish)
   5 dolphins (who live in the wild)
   6 the fish
   7 the frisbee
   8 the dolphins'

3 1 a   2 b
   3 a   4 a
   5 a   6 b

4 2 T   3 T
   4 F   5 F
   6 F

UNITS 1–3
WRITING

1 Answers will vary.

2 Answers will vary.

3 Answers will vary. Some possible answers:
Introduction: e
Main part: a, b, f, g, h
Conclusion: c, d

4 Answers will vary.

UNITS 4–6
WRITING

1 just in time, after a short time, in 1947, at first, finally, in 1966, by then, nowadays

2 Answers will vary.

3 2 in 1946
3 testing a new piece of radar technology (called "magnetron")
4 (in 1947) a large machine almost two meters tall and over 350 kilos
5 became smaller and easier to control, became available for domestic use
6 in 1947 (for places where large quantities of food needed to be cooked quickly), in 1966 (for domestic use)
7 Students may add more information. Possible answers: in homes (all over the world), restaurants, railroad cars; for heating or preparing food
8 Students may add more information. Possible answers: made cooking quicker and easier

4 Answers will vary.

UNITS 7–9
WRITING

1 Answers will vary.

2 Answers will vary.

3 Where to go   8
A short history   4, 5, 6
Location and population 2, 3

4 Answers will vary. Possible answer:
Location and population
A short history
Where to go

UNITS 10–12
WRITING

1 1 Dolphins...
2 By keeping...
3 However,...
4 In my opinion,...

2 Answers will vary.

3 Answers will vary.